---
endorsements

Having been a counselor or over 30 years, I have found the tools as laid out in *Boardroom of the Inner Man* of great value. Not only have I used these guidelines for many, many hurt and wounded people but also for my own journey into wholeness. I highly recommend these very valuable and practical ways of seeing the picture of your personality to everyone interested in the journey toward wholeness.

Susanne Fengler
Original co-author of The Boardroom of the Inner Man, Australia

Boardroom of the Inner Man is a fresh and creative way of understanding the dynamics of our internal world and has quickly become an essential tool in helping me engage with God at a deeper level. Julie explains this concept with her usual warmth and wit, and with plenty of helpful (and honest) insights from her own personal spiritual journey. I really encourage you to read this book!

Vicky Schulz
Director of European School of Supernatural Life, Gravesend, Kent, UK

I believe the greatest issue in the church today is the lack of intimacy. Many believers wrestle with how to hear God, how to walk close with Him, and how to experience His presence in our daily lives. There is so much noise around us, but more to the point, inside us. Julie Appleyard has written a clear and practical guide to help us cut through the noise—so we can hear and know Him. Julie writes with insight and grace; her words resonate with our own story. *Boardroom of the Inner Man* is an invitation to journey with Holy Spirit into wholeness. It is an invitation to a fuller life of confidence in God's good love. I was encouraged through its pages and believe you will be as well!

Jason Clark
Director of A Family Story Ministries, NC, USA
Author of Prone to Love, God Is (Not) In Control, and Untamed

Julie's book, *Boardroom of the Inner Man*, is a true gift for anyone pursuing their destiny. God wants to empower us with His Spirit of truth, which is a Spirit of power, love, and a sound mind. A sound mind is a free gift from God, but it is our own responsibility to cultivate it.

I am a catalyst for change, and have seen many people and organizations being restored to their original design, but not many renew their way of thinking. Without this shift in thinking the behavior does not change, and neither do the results.

In this book, Julie takes you step-by-step through her own journey to develop self-control in relationship with the Holy Spirit. She explains how to cultivate your decision- making so that you can sustain the wholeness to which we have been restored, by Jesus. Seize this opportunity, and let the Holy Spirit guide you in renewing your thinking.

Arjan Visser
Change Agent, Managing Partner Business Revivalists,
The Netherlands

When the Apostle Paul wrote about grace and peace, he could have had Julie in mind. While both of these qualities seem to be extremely rare in the world in which we live, Julie breathes them into every aspect of her life and into all of her relationships. I believe the key to these qualities being so evident in her is due to her personal, intimate walk with God. In *Boardroom of the Inner Man*, Julie gives down-to-earth insights into hearing from Daddy, practicing His presence, and living out of a place of peace in a world that is getting increasingly more chaotic.

Lowell McNaney
**Senior Pastor, Crossroads United Methodist Church,
Concord, NC, USA
Author of Fuel for the Journey**

Anothen Business Series
BOARDROOM OF THE INNER MAN
© 2017 Julie Appleyard
All rights reserved

Cover design by Keira Prowd, Prowd Design
Author's Photo by Whitney Gray, www.whitneygrayphotography.com
Formatting by Reddovedesign.com

Unless otherwise noted, all Scripture quotations are taken from the HCSB®, Copyright © 1999, 2000, 2002, 2003, 2009 by Holman Bible Publishers. Used by permission. HCSB® is a federally registered trademark of Holman Bible Publishers.

Scripture quotations are taken from the Holy Bible, New Living Translation, copyright ©1996, 2004, 2007, 2013, 2015 by Tyndale House Foundation. Used by permission of Tyndale House Publishers, Inc., Carol Stream, Illinois 60188. All rights reserved.

Scripture quotations marked (NIV) are taken from the Holy Bible, New International Version®, NIV®. Copyright © 1973, 1978, 1984, 2011 by Biblica, Inc.™ Used by permission of Zondervan. All rights reserved worldwide. www.zondervan.com The "NIV" and "New International Version" are trademarks registered in the United States Patent and Trademark Office by Biblica, Inc.™

'Scriptures and additional materials quoted marked (GNB) are from the Good News Bible © 1994 published by the Bible Societies/HarperCollins Publishers Ltd UK, Good News Bible© American Bible Society 1966, 1971, 1976, 1992. Used with permission.'

The Interlinear Bible, Hebrew-Greek-English by Jay P Green, Sr. General Editor and Translator, Second Edition copyright 1986 by Hendrickson Publishers, Peabody, Massachusetts. Used by permission. All rights reserved.

ISBN 978-1-946503-01-5
To order more books or resources contact
info@anothen.co

Boardroom Of The Inner Man

"I pray that He may grant you, according to the riches of His glory, to be strengthened with power in the inner man through His Spirit, and that the Messiah may dwell in your hearts through faith. I pray that you, being firmly rooted and established in love, may be able to comprehend with all the saints what is the length and width, height and depth of God's love, and to know the Messiah's love that surpasses knowledge, so you may be filled with all the fullness of God"
(Ephesians 3:16-18, HCSB).

Julie Appleyard

dedication

For Granny, who showed me what it looked like to revere God;
For Grandpa, who showed me what it looked like to have radical faith;
For Nana, who showed me what it looked like to be a servant;
For Pa, who showed me what it looked like to overcome;
For Mum, who taught me (among other things) the value of perseverance;
For Dad, who taught me the value of a sound mind;
For Dane and Bella, Jessie-Naree, and Alex-Anne, who's zeal for, and faith in the Lord inspire me every day;
And for Mark, who is my greatest champion, always!

God, I thank You for all of them, every day—for these are the shoulders upon which I stand.

Table of Contents

Dedication	vii
Foreword by Kim Beaumont	11
Introduction	13
Chapter One: A Meeting Has Been Called	19
Chapter Two: The Mind	31
Chapter Three: The Heart	51
Chapter Four: The Emotions	75
Chapter Five: The Conscience	95
Chapter Six: The Will	111
Chapter Seven: The Human Spirit	125
Chapter Eight: The Body	145
Chapter Nine: The Holy Spirit CEO	161
Acknowledgements	177

foreword

The power of God's promises, combined with our intentional and intimate connection with God, is key to us being fully who God created us to be. *Boardroom of the Inner Man* is strategic and gives clarity to that mission precisely.

Julie colorfully illustrates the explanation of our *inner boardroom* clearly and succinctly. Her conversations with Holy Spirit, and her different board members, make me feel *sane*, knowing that there are others who have self-talk that is like my own. She has been given a strong revelation of how lies are built up in our minds and hearts, until they finally become our *false* truth; and how the power of real, Divine truth can overcome this and help us walk in complete freedom.

I love that Julie has included her journal entries; they helped me to immediately connect with her as a *real* person, one who is authentic and vulnerable about her inner journey, while still conducting an *outer* ministry position and life style. These journal entries and stories from her life enable us to relate to a perfectly imperfect daughter, who loves God, and is still trying to figure out what that looks like—just like all of us.

Boardroom of the Inner Man is a tool that can be used by full-time ministers (as an effective tool), or fellow Kingdom Seekers as a method of drawing closer to His heart. Whether you're a CEO, a stay at home mom, or a college student, this is the kind of book that should be read once a year; it will help us to realign and connect with the One who created us in the first place, bringing us back to our glorious original design!

Pastor Kim Beaumont, Bethel Church, Redding, California.

introduction

"Get up, sleeper, and rise up from the dead, and the Messiah will shine on you…" (Ephesians 5:14, HCSB).

Journal Entry, 26th August 2003: *"Lord, Easter Convention seems so far away, and too long to wait for. I don't want to keep living my Christianity on the smell of an oily rag—on memories of feelings and emotions that come once a year…the personal growth course that my friend Amie has been talking about sounds helpful. If it can teach me things that will deepen my relationship with You then it is worth pursuing. I **don't** want it to become just another tried and failed means of stroking my emotions…"*

Perhaps you've been where I was. Perhaps you are there still—wondering if there really could be more to this whole Christian lifestyle than the endless cycle of church, small groups, committee meetings and social events. Not that there's anything intrinsically *wrong* with any of those things, but if that's all that could be expected from the Christian life—the *victorious* Christian life that I'd heard so much about all my years—then I was dissatisfied.

I hungered for the type of relationship with God that I believed others had; the type of relationship where I could sit down over a cup of tea or coffee and have deep and meaningful conversations about all the things I've struggled with in my life. I longed for the type of relationship in which I'd know beyond a shadow of a doubt that I could hear His voice. Audibly.

I wanted a flesh and blood relationship with a flesh and blood Jesus that I could see, hear, touch and discern with my physical senses. I wanted a relationship in which there was no questioning His reality, and no questioning the validity of the connection and rapport I had with Him. I just didn't know *how* to have that kind of relationship with Him, and at the time I was not even convinced that He was that interested in having *any* kind of relationship with me.

The fact is, He created us to have that kind of relationship with Him. Most of us just don't have the first clue as to how that is supposed to look. We follow the rules set in place by the established Church and wonder why it doesn't lead to the kind of heartfelt connection that we long for from our Creator. There is a part of us that is deeply asleep— that part of us that was designed to interact with Him on a daily basis—and the sad thing is that we don't even know what we are missing out on. We aren't even aware that this kind of relationship is within our grasp. We just let the possibility of Him pass us by, not recognizing the precious treasure that it is, and never knowing how good it could be *if we only knew...*

Throughout these pages, you will read selected journal entries that reflect the cry of my heart as I travelled. I hope that in sharing these conversations I've had with the Lord in writing, you will gather enough courage to begin having some of your own. I must confess to having some hesitation in going down this path, for two reasons: first, I do *not* want to soap-box or work out my frustrations and growing pains on those whom I am honored to have read these chapters. That would be entirely selfish.

I *do* want to leave a trail of breadcrumbs, so to speak, for you to follow. I want to encourage you to take a step of your own, then another and another, until you are running solidly in your own journey. Perhaps you'll overtake me and leave your own trail of breadcrumbs for *me* to follow. That would be cool. *That* would give purpose to my writing.

Second, I *don't* want to suggest that my way is the best way or the only way to pursue a deeper relationship with Jesus; it's just *my* way, the way He engaged *me*, the way that I have followed and that has led me to where I am today. When you read my journal entries, please do not assume that God will only talk to you in the same way He talks to me. He might, but then again, He might use better illustrations, much grander imagery, and more complex ideas to engage your imagination and draw you closer to Himself.

That's the beauty of our personal walk with God—He will speak to you in ways that *you* will understand, beginning right where you are and coaxing you forward…always forward. I would like to offer my journey as a catalyst for your own, to point out the paths and the stepping stones that I have found trustworthy along the way, and to be the person who goes ahead of you, who is able to say "Hey! This is cool! And it's *safe* to stand here, because it lines up with Scripture!"

THE INVITATION

When our son, Dane, was little, maybe twelve months old, it was really fun to let him taste new foods. He was a curious little man, and often would grab from whatever we were eating, whether it was appropriate for a one-year-old to eat or not. Have you ever watched a child that young experience a new taste? They experience it with their whole body. There's a short, quick wobble that starts with an expression of surprise and travels from their head, all the way down their spine. You wait, breathlessly for a moment or two for the verdict. They will either immediately pull toward them or push away the offered food, depending on whether they liked the experience or not.

"Taste and see that the Lord is good. How happy is the man who takes refuge in Him!" (Psalm 34:8 HCSB). This is an invitation to *experience* Him. To taste something is to experience it. I can look at the nectarine in the fruit basket and appreciate that it *looks* ripe enough to eat. I can *touch* it and appreciate the cool texture of its skin and softness of its flesh. I can *smell* it and appreciate its fragrance. I cannot, however,

appreciate its sweetness, its juiciness, its nutritional value, or its hunger satisfying abilities unless I also *taste* it. If I don't taste it, I don't experience it fully; I can only say I have *partially* experienced it.

To taste is to dive right in, throw caution to the wind and put yourself in a position where you are fully aware that you might not like what you are about to experience. Come on now—who *hasn't* ever tasted something that they wished they hadn't? You'll never know, however, until you stick your tongue on it and taste it. The best part about this invitation is that we have the assurance that we will *love* it, because it is scriptural and biblical…God said it in His word. What more do you want?

The Lord offers Himself—"Taste! Experience! Dive right in!" Then He waits for a moment, breathless, and watches for our response. We will either pull Him close or push Him away, depending on what it is we have been taught to believe we *should* feel about the experience…I never want to push Him away!

When I was first introduced to the *Boardroom of the Inner Man* through a close friend, it was an invitation to taste. I saw her relationship with God evolve before me into the kind of relationship that I longed for myself. I had seen the fruit in her life, I had watched her growth, and marveled with her as she described what she had tasted when she accepted the invitation for herself. I couldn't live out my Christian life or my relationship with God vicariously through her, however. There came a moment where I had to commit to tasting for myself; to dive right in and immerse myself in my own experience of who God is, and who He wanted to be for me. So I began attending "Thursday Group"—the somewhat innocent and very harmless title given to the group that would introduce me to the wonderful, beautiful, amazing, and eternally indescribable God I had been serving all my life.

Tasting something *this* good usually results in *telling someone* that they simply *must* try the nectarine! Every now and then, you come across someone who simply doesn't like nectarines—but if your experience has been *that* good you will not give up on your persuading arguments so easily.

The concept of the *Boardroom of the Inner Man* was what started me on my own personal journey of spiritual growth and discovery. I was, as I have said, intrigued by my friend's experience and was hungry to find out more. The first venture into my own inner boardroom was fascinating and revealing; I have not stopped delving into the mysteries that God constantly presents to me. Exploring my boardroom drove me into the Word of God, and consequently deeper into His heart and His character. I've learned that God speaks to me directly, and I've learned to cultivate the skill of listening to the still small voice of the Holy Spirit that never stops speaking. The more you pay attention to His voice, the clearer and more recognizable it becomes.

I do want to include a disclaimer, at this point. I am not, nor do I profess to have the depth of knowledge of a doctor of psychology or psychiatry. I have had no formal training in the art of counseling beyond what I have learned, informally, through my years of working in the health industry as a nurse and midwife and in the ministry as I have served within the church in varying capacities. My language and views reflect a perspective honed by my years of interacting with the Lord, and with others with whom I have journeyed, as we seek to address our own issues and face life's challenges.

This disclaimer aside, I have discovered great value in rolling up my sleeves and getting into the trenches of life with others. Real life, along with all its inconveniences and ill timed circumstances, does not always lend itself to the neatness of the counselor or therapist's office. Although I greatly value that approach, there are times you must deal with the mess of the moment and get on with life. I have found that the tools the boardroom's concepts have to offer are invaluable in sorting through life's unpredictable challenges.

I still have (many, and sometimes lengthy) periods of dysfunctionality, even after knowing all of this. Now, however, I have the tools and the knowledge to troubleshoot and identify which of my board members is struggling to submit to the Holy Spirit. I now ask, "Where is His conviction? What voice has taken the floor in my boardroom?" Once I can identify those things, I then know how to quickly bring my boardroom back into alignment with what He wants.

My prayer for you as you read these pages is that you will discover for yourself the brilliance, the magnificence, the everlasting *loveliness* of your Savior; that you will come to know His voice as well as you know your own; and that you will discover for yourself the absolute joy of learning to submit every area of your life to His Lordship and guidance.

chapter one

A Meeting Has Been Called

"It is the glory of God to conceal a matter, and the glory of kings to investigate a matter." (Proverbs 25:2, HCSB).

Journal Entry, Good Friday, 18th April 2003. 10:00 p.m.: *"For years—my whole life, in fact—I have felt like a failure as a Christian. I've seen God work; I have been moved by His power; I need no proof of God's existence—but I've always felt on the outside. As if I can look, but not touch; it's like eating something that I know is supposed to be sweet, but not being able to taste it. Reading descriptions, seeing how others react, I can almost fool myself into believing that I have actually experienced the sweetness for myself—but I know I really haven't.*

*"Living by faith, to me, always meant being in Christian work full time and not being paid for it. By that definition, I have been living by faith for the past seven years. Regardless of how spiritual that sounds, I still feel empty. I still don't really **know** Christ. Hearing His name stirs in me a restlessness I can't define. Hunger on the one hand but, lately, mostly frustration that I don't know Him as I should, or as I really want to.*

"Hearing Charles Price explain, tonight at the conference, that living by faith is not "working for no pay" at all, but instead, it is living each moment in Christ by putting one's faith in someone bigger and stronger

than oneself and carrying out His work in His strength. He told us that it is actually a sin to not live by faith, and that made me realize I had a lot of thinking to do, some repenting to do, some confessing to do…and some healing and growing to do. I also need to change my mindset on how I live my life—or, more specifically, how I live my Christian life. I will never live a victorious Christian life if I only put my energies into doing all the right things and saying all the right words…I must, moment by moment, put my tiny little bit of faith into my big, strong God and submit to Him always."

That was the Australian autumn of 2003, at Easter time. We were camping up in Belgrave Heights, a quaint little mountain town on the outskirts of Melbourne that was host to the Keswick Convention Centre. Every Easter and Christmas several thousand Christians from all over Victoria, and some from New South Wales and South Australia, would converge in this little town for a week of solid exegetical Bible teaching and good old-fashioned Christian fellowship. For me, it was a comfortably familiar place, laced with fond memories and an atmosphere of sturdy, foundational truths and beliefs that had helped shape my Christian character, and the character of countless others over the years. The journal entry above was squeezed into the pages between the sermon notes of Charles Price and Dr. Gary Inrig; I had no idea of the magnitude of the journey the Lord would take me on from that point.

That one entry captured the cry of my heart— "There has to be more to it than this!" You see, I had been a Christian for as long as I could remember. I do not remember a time when I was not encouraged to say my prayers at night, or grace before dinner. I cut my teeth in church, attended Sunday school, and heard Bible stories from before I knew how to speak. My conversion experience had been at that very campground around twenty-six years earlier, when I was five-years-old.

My granny and I celebrated Christmas that year at the convention, staying in Uncle Norm's little caravan—I could probably even lead you to the almost-exact place. I prayed "the prayer" and had what I now recognize as my first encounter with God. After Granny had led me in the prayer, and I had conscientiously repeated it, line-by-line, I sat in her lap in the cramped little caravan; there was just enough room for a double bed on one end, a small table with bench seats on the other, a "kitchen" with a gas cook-top and about a square foot of counter space in the middle. I remember opening my eyes, feeling surprised that everything in the caravan looked the same. With my hands tightly folded under my chin, I looked up at her and exclaimed; "Granny! I think He did!"

"Did what?" she asked.

"Come into my heart!" Granny laughed as she lifted me down off her knee so she could "put the kettle on."

When I told her that He had hugged me; she said "Did He, darlin'?" Then she smiled, hugged me, and sent me to bed.

I remember lying in bed, watching Granny with her cup of coffee in one hand and her Bible open on her knee; I was feeling very different, even though everything looked so much the same. I drifted off to sleep sometime after Granny put down her Bible and picked up her knitting.

Fast forward to me as a grown woman with a husband and three children of my own, and somehow I recognized that there was something, or *someone*, that I had missed along the way. My cozy memory of asking Jesus into my heart, just over the crest of the hill all those years ago, did not match my current inner turmoil. As I put my journal away that night, I asked the Lord to please, *please* intervene somehow. I had the very unnerving sense that I would self-destruct, or worse—settle into a lukewarm, mediocre expression of my faith and Christianity—if He did not reveal Himself to me in some tangible way.

One day, not too long after, as I was sitting with my friend Amie in my lounge-room, she started talking about a topic that intrigued me. Amie and her husband Bill were associate pastors on staff at the church where we were pastoring, at the time. She had been attending a women's Bible study at a church in a neighboring suburb and was quite excited about the things she was learning. I was intrigued because she was talking about Jesus like she actually *had* a real relationship with Him, not just like she "had a relationship with Him." The distinction was small, and I almost missed it, having been around churches and church jargon all my life. There was, however, a tone to her voice, a look in her eye, and an expression on her face that caught my attention and prompted me to ask a question...

"Wait—you said 'When you asked Jesus'...do you mean He *answered* you? What did He say?" She paused and looked at me, recognizing my hunger. She had said it so effortlessly; like she was telling me about a conversation she had engaged in with her mother or her husband or anyone else for that matter. What caught my attention was that *she expected Jesus to answer her!*

This one simple comment, during a regular conversation with a friend, changed the course of my spiritual journey, putting me on an entirely different path. In one brilliant instance, the possibility that Jesus would *want* to answer me reignited the sparks within me I thought had long been quenched. Amie willingly explained to me in more detail how she was learning to hear the voice of the Lord, and how her faith was growing, along with her ability to hear Him. Needless to say, I began attending the study group with her each week, and thus began a new phase of my spiritual growth, along with the realization that God wants to talk with me *much* more than I want to hear Him.

A World-Changing Concept...

You know how, sometimes, God brings people into your life that have a lasting impact? Susanne Fengler was one of those people. Susanne led the study group that I began attending with my friend, Amie, and the principles I learned under her teaching have kept my faith growing strong fourteen years later. The concept of the *Boardroom of the Inner Man* is one of inner healing and spiritual growth; it had, at that stage, been taught in Australia by Susanne and her husband, Daniel for the previous ten years or more in the counseling room, in study groups and in seminars. This tool incorporates many of the same familiar concepts as many other inner-healing tools of which you might have heard. (Recently, this has been published in e-book form, and can be purchased online under the title "A Personal Boardroom? Sorting Out the 7 Members of Your Personality" by Pastor Sharon White, Daniel and Susanne Fengler.)

Daniel and Susanne Fengler came from America to Australia in 1974 as secondary school teachers and taught in the Australian high school system for thirteen years. They had been ministers and counselors for over twenty years and, in 2008, moved into coaching and mentoring as their main ministry. At the time of this writing they are now retired, but still actively coaching and mentoring whomever the Lord sees fit to send their way.

During their twenty years of working with people in crisis, they began to see patterns emerging in the way people lived their lives. They recognized that different aspects of someone's personality were *in control*, while other weaker parts were under developed, or almost non-existent. This is not to say that everyone has multiple personality disorder; rather, it was a startling observation made during thousands of counseling sessions about the way we function as human beings. In the context of the Christian counseling room, these tools were developed to help bring people to wholeness in Christ, and became known to them and the people they counseled as *The Boardroom of the Inner Man*. As Daniel and Susanne watched the fascinating reality of people's inner struggles and the commonalities between them, they came to realize that when people used these tools as part of their everyday relationship with the Lord, many of the crises they would face in life became less of a crisis, and more of a challenge to be faced with Jesus at their side.

The first group sessions were taught in a small group setting, gathering together four or five women who were all at a similar stage in their counseling journey. Those five women invited others, who invited others, and as the concept took off, the group grew to over forty women. Since that first pilot group, *The Boardroom of the Inner Man* has been taught to men and women of all ages and stages of spiritual maturity, with measurable spiritual growth reported by participants, as well as the people who walk the Christian journey closest to them. Learning these skills opens the door to a vibrant and God-centered spiritual journey that will not just whet your appetite for more of Him, but will launch you into a life of faith and dependency on Him like you have never known before.

Using the boardroom concept is *one way* of looking at our inner struggles, with the view to bringing us to healing and wholeness in Christ, which, in turn, develops the relationship with Him for which we were made. Part of the reason we struggle is because we don't know what is going on in our inner world; it certainly became very clear that this is why I was struggling. By recognizing all the parts in the whole boardroom, I learned to value how God made me—every *member* is valuable and needed to function in wholeness. When I understood this, I was able to develop a better balance between each of the members of my boardroom—I learned to recognize my own weaknesses and strengths, and in observing the interaction between those members, I could help each one come under the Lordship of Jesus, thus finding and sustaining the peace that only He can give. I was able step into His view of me, rather than living by my own self-focused worldly perspectives.

This concept of an *inner boardroom* is not difficult to grasp. Even if we have never experienced a board meeting for ourselves, we've all seen the dramatizations on television and in the movies. There is always an overbearing member, who yells and thumps the table authoritatively with his clenched fist in order to get his point across; the bored-looking member who twirls his pencil and looks at his watch periodically; the CEO, who either commands attention and dominates by his very presence, or demands it in dictatorial ways; then there are the members who appear to have no say at all, but who scurry to do the bidding of everyone else. We've all seen what can happen if the board rejects the authority of the CEO. We're all aware of the damage that can be done if the board does not operate in unity.

The same is true with each one of us. Inside each of us are *board members* that must learn to work together, submitting to the CEO who, in keeping with the concept analogy, is the Holy Spirit. He will be referred to as Holy Spirit CEO throughout the rest of this book. Perhaps you are familiar with some of these characters? Our modern-day poets and songwriters have captured this concept well. The lyrics to many songs, and even our everyday language, reflect that we are aware of more than one aspect of our inner self. For example, have you ever said something along the lines of "My head says one thing, but my heart tells me something different?" Maybe you have said something more like, "My conscience is really beating me up over that decision!"; or, "My heart's just not in it!"; or "I don't have the will power…"

My everyday language reflected all of those types of statements, and more. The understanding of my own inner workings was limited and frighteningly inaccurate. I *thought* I was doing okay. Yes, I could get a little emotional at times, but wasn't that just the lot of every woman on the planet? I was prideful in my assumption that I knew enough of the Bible to get me by, but I was still painfully aware of that missing piece.

CRUNCH TIME…

There came a moment where I had to decide. Did I really want to discover the missing piece? Or was I content to live with the tension that the missing piece created? For me, it was a no-brainer; I was tired of living with the tension, so I took a risk, sat down with my journal one day and asked the Lord a simple question. Then I got brave enough to sit and listen for His answer. That conversation is recorded below…

Journal Entry, 26th August, 2003 (later): *"I have asked You a few times, "What does my boardroom look like?" The impression I get is that it's crowded—it's full of things and people, to the point where I can't move without crashing into someone or something. And, every object has legs—so they can move themselves around and maneuver into the most prominent position they can find. I feel I have no control over any of it.*

"Now all this sounds fantastical to me—and I know that my imagination is, at best, overactive and, at worst, misleading (too powerful and uncontrolled). I am struggling to accept that this is a true picture; I do not doubt it could be from You and, therefore, be very accurate—I just don't want the sugar coated version; I don't want to ignore or cover up anything by imagining things differently than what they are. So, let's assume, that having asked You for a picture, You actually gave me one and that this impression is accurate, and from You. All of these things with legs (and supposedly minds) of their own need to go, obviously. How do I "un-crowd" my boardroom? Somehow, breaking all those legs seems unnecessarily destructive!

"ASK THEM TO LEAVE."

To ask them to move on out of there seems too simple and ineffective. What happens when they walk right back in again?

"ASK THEM AGAIN!"

I don't know if I have that much patience.

"PATIENCE WILL COME…"

*"(So, when I asked them to leave, they retreated to seats and bleachers around the board table, with the understanding that they are spectators only. Now I have a great crowd of things with legs, and people, watching how my board meetings are conducted. I think I would have preferred that they left the boardroom altogether! Lord, I can't find You in this crowd. I think I catch glimpses—I want to see You, unobstructed and unhindered…Show me where **You** are…)"*

Are you intrigued? Are you ready to take a risk? Are you brave enough to taste and see what the Lord has for you, and experience your own boardroom encounter?

Imagine with me, if you will, a boardroom; it can be as simple or as opulent as you want it to be. There is a large table, surrounded by eight chairs. To the right of the CEO's chair sits the Heart, and next to that, the Mind, and to the left of the CEO sits the Conscience, then the Emotions. These four, in the dysfunctional boardroom scenario, are what I call the "CEO wanna-bes". They vie for the position of Chairman. They each want to be the one to call the shots. For each individual person, it will vary as to which of these members carries the most authority.

For some, the Mind is the strongest member. The Mind wants logic and rational thought to rule, and it can be very forceful in its opinions; so too, the Conscience. The Conscience's catch-cry is "should", "must", "ought!" and it can bully the other board members into a decision they might not otherwise make if it is given an audience.

For others, the Emotions are the dominant voice, as they seem to run rampant and throw their weight around in the Boardroom, demanding that they be heard and obeyed right-now-this-minute. In actual fact, the Emotions are messengers from the Heart. They were never designed to control or rule in the Boardroom, but in their unregenerate and dysfunctional state of being, that is the goal they pursue.

Perhaps it's the Heart that wants to be in control. The Heart always wants to be heard, and it believes it should also always be obeyed. The Heart will not give in easily to the logical, rational arguments of the Mind.

The other members seated at the table are the Will—who is a bit of a floating voter, following the loudest or most dominant voice in the moment; the Body, who tends to be the whipping-boy, and is very much at the mercy of the whims of the other members, carrying within itself all the stresses and tensions generated by the dysfunctional activity of its cohorts; and the Human Spirit, who has largely abdicated its authority to whoever and whatever will argue against it, because no one in the boardroom will listen to it anyway, much less submit to it, or recognize any authority it carries.

So where is the Holy Spirit CEO, you might ask? In the dysfunctional boardroom, the Holy Spirit CEO is largely ignored. The Holy Spirit is a gentleman; therefore He will not dominate or demand authority that is not freely given to Him. If He is not wanted, He will step back until He is asked to step in again; it takes very little imagination to see the consequences of the way this board operates. Things may hold together for a short while, true, but in the long run there will be a trail of destruction and more failed attempts than successful ones at making productive decisions.

To clarify, some of us think we work quite well in our dysfunctional state. I know I did! Upon closer inspection, though, we come to realize that when anyone other than the Holy Spirit assumes the role of CEO, there will *always* be some part of us that is beaten down, under-developed or immature and, therefore, ineffective. We become spiritually unhealthy which, in turn, means we are not operating at our best, the way God intended.

The concept of the *Boardroom of the Inner Man* that Susanne and her husband Daniel were given by the Lord to use as a tool in the counseling room during their years of ministry has helped me stay strong in my everyday walk with Him. I was able to identify some of the reasons why I struggled to hear from Him, and how to break through those barriers. I found out that my Mind, my Emotions, my Heart, my Conscience, my Body, my own Human Spirit, and my Will all play a vital part in being fully submitted to Him. I have learned that, sometimes, one part could rebel while everything else wanted to submit, and vice versa.

I began an actual dialogue with Jesus that has developed, over the years, into an ever-deepening love-friendship with my Creator. I *know* His voice; it is one of the most precious sounds in the world to me. The embrace I felt in the caravan when I was five years old is familiar again, and I have learned to trust Him in ways I could have never imagined I would need, or even want, to trust! I still often tell Him, "There has to be more than this!" The tone, however, is different now, less desperate and more eager; because I am now convinced that He wants me to have more than what I currently have, even more than I want to have it.

There is a verse in Proverbs, 25:2, which says, *"It is the glory of God to conceal a matter and the glory of kings to investigate a matter" (HCSB)*. I have come to believe that there are many things that have been *hidden* for us to find; that He delights in us when we ask Him questions and search Him out. The more we seek Him, the more we find Him; it's a never ending journey because, as much as we discover about His nature and character, there is infinitely more to yet be discovered. As the old Chinese saying goes, "A journey of a thousand miles begins with a single step." So, are you ready to embark on your own journey? Let's go meet the members of *your* boardroom...

chapter two

THE MIND

"Do not be conformed to this age, but be transformed by the renewing of your mind, so that you may discern what is the good, pleasing and perfect will of God." (Romans 12:2, HCSB).

Journal Entry, 1st November, 2003: "Lord, how do You see my Mind? What is it really like?

"Wow! You just showed me that my Mind is like a huge screen TV, which is constantly on; it has a self-remote-control system so it can switch from one channel to another on whatever whim it pleases; it can control its own volume, too. Even in sleep mode, it plays inane sounds and pictures from the past—sometimes it treats the Heart and replays some of its favorite memories. Mostly, though, it just tunes into whatever is interesting at the time; or annoys the rest of the Boardroom by flicking from one channel to another when it should be focused on one thing.

"My Mind is like a TV with a mind of its own…that's bizarre! Lord, how do I begin to override the self-remote-control thing?

"ONE OF THE FRUITS OF THE SPIRIT IS SELF-CONTROL"

"So, I need to spend a lot of time working with the Holy Spirit and my Mind in order to gain self-control in this area…"

To fully understand the function of the mind, it becomes necessary to delve into a little bit of psychology. Psychology, in many Christian circles, has been debunked as being invalid to the Christian life and mindset, but there are some foundational truths that can be substantiated in Biblical terms. If we work from the premise that Jesus claimed to *be* the Truth, then Truth remains Truth, no matter who tries to lay claim to it. So, we will be exploring some psychological arguments in this chapter, as they pertain to *the* Truth of who Jesus is and who He claimed to be. I would like to remind the reader that I do not have a degree in Psychology, and this is purely a layman's understanding of the topic, described in layman's terms as I have gained understanding through my time with the Lord. Please bear this in mind as you read.

THE UNREGENERATE MIND.

Let's look at the Mind as it is *before* it has submitted itself to the authority of the Holy Spirit—the unregenerate Mind. The unregenerate Mind likes to think it is and wants to *be*, in control of everything; it uses logic and reason to develop ideas, make decisions, and to coerce the other board members into following what it wants.

The unregenerate Mind tries to keep lists and records for itself, so it can keep track of everything and, therefore, be aware of everything. There must be a reason for all things, and it must be able to justify every decision it makes and every action it takes. If something cannot be explained logically or rationally, then that something either does not exist, or is of no consequence to the day-to-day operation of the Mind.

The unregenerate Mind likes to be in control. When it is not in control, it starts to look for reasons *why* it is not in control and then begins to blame the other board members, rationalizing why it *should* be in control. The Mind can get quite belligerent in its assertions, rarely allowing any other board member a voice, unless that board member can present a logical, rational argument for its case.

The implications of this kind of thinking are that the Mind repeatedly ignores the other board members, especially if there is no *logical* explanation for the behavior or argument that has surfaced. When the unregenerate Mind is unable to rationalize the behavior of the board, it is reminded that it is unaware of, and not in control of, all the information. When the other board members are ignored, particularly those board members who want the position of CEO, they can get a pretty strong attitude of their own. The end result is a power struggle between the Mind and the rest of the board.

We may feel stressed when the Mind is not in control because of the extra pressure the Mind puts on the competing board members to come up with a rational explanation, which they may be unwilling or unable to do because they remain unheard. The non-competing board members either pick sides or bow out of the discussion altogether, thus resulting in indecisiveness and inaction until the Mind gains the upper hand again. "Peace of Mind" is not obtained unless the Mind regains control and can explain everything logically and rationally once again.

The Developing Mind.

The Mind, as we grow and develop from childhood, creates neuro pathways, or patterns of thinking, that become a default setting as we get older. Learned behaviors and actions such as walking, talking, eating, reading, playing a musical instrument or a particular sport all fall into this category. Repeating those actions over and over creates pathways in the brain and can be described as "muscle memory."

We do not think about how we must perform these learned tasks. We cannot "forget" how to walk or talk unless the brain sustains some form of severe injury; in such cases we must "re-learn," or recreate the neuro-pathways that help the action of walking or talking become second nature again. In the same way, when we collect and review the same or similar thought patterns repeatedly, the brain creates a neuro-pathway that reflects that pattern of thinking.

When the Mind is required to think through something, it searches for the pathway or the pattern that most closely reflects the scenario it has been presented with previously. When it finds the pattern, it slides right into that groove and follows it to the end.

What do I mean by this? Let's say that as a child, you were never encouraged to say what you thought. You might have had a domineering parent that lived by the adage "children should be seen and not heard." To survive, your Mind creates the pathway of thinking that says, "You'd better keep your mouth shut! People get angry when you say what you think." Whether that thought pattern was truthful or not, that is the pattern that helped you survive. Whenever you find yourself in a situation that requires that you say what you think, there is a well-worn thought pathway that says, "Keep your mouth shut!"

Conversely, you may have been encouraged at every turn to share what you thought. The pathway of thinking that forms here is, "What I have to say is important." When you are faced with a situation where no one is interested in what you have to say, the reaction becomes "Wait a minute! You should listen to me!"

All our lives we are fed information, but not all of that information is truth. Some of the information that we receive is faulty. Therefore, many of the pathways of thinking that we have formed over our lifetime are faulty. For instance, how many of us remember the cruel words spoken to us on the school playground by kids that were older and bigger than ourselves? Some of us have carried around those words and their resulting thought processes for many years. As long as the Mind is convinced that those words are *truth*, it will hold onto the faulty thought processes that go along with them. Rather than correct the thinking, the Mind will justify and rationalize its familiar thought patterns and try to convince the other board members that it is right to think that way.

When the Mind *can* recognize the words as not true, however, it will habitually process its thought patterns *opposite* to the original faulty patterns. The opposite of a lie is not always truth. If I was told, but did not believe, that I was ugly and could never be beautiful, then I might process that information in terms of the opposite— "No! I *am* beautiful, and I'm gonna' prove it to the world!" I swing to the opposite extreme and begin to think I'm "all that and a little bit more," which in this distorted form is still *not* truth.

In my endeavor to be perceived as beautiful, I actually cultivate some very unlovely attitudes and thought pathways that will only serve to convince the people around me that no matter what I look like on the outside, I am not a beautiful person.

In Romans 12:2, Paul says *"Do not be conformed to the patterns of this world, but be **transformed by the renewing of your mind** so that you may discern the good, pleasing and perfect will of God." (HCSB, emphasis mine)*. What I believe he is saying here is "identify and get rid of your faulty ways of thinking! Realign your thought patterns to God's way of thinking." He is warning us not to think the way the world thinks, and not to continue thinking the things we always thought were true, but aren't.

How the Mind Discerns...

So, how do we identify our own faulty ways of thinking? Given that the unregenerate Mind likes to be in control, it is very difficult for it to just switch ways of thinking without a little bit of work. Here is where it can get very interesting.

Our Mind is not just a rational, logical thinker; it is also the interface between the physical world that we exist in and the spiritual realm. Our Mind interprets the messages of touch and temperature, smell, sound, sight and taste that our Body is constantly sending us, working in conjunction with the Body to process that information. The

Mind can also judge distance, height, and depth; it interprets this information about our physical environment, and we are able to respond, accordingly, because of that ability. Put your hand on something hot and your Mind is the one to send the message, "Ouch! Hot!", causing the Body to pull the hand away almost instantaneously.

The Mind also constantly receives information about the spiritual realm from our Human Spirit and the Holy Spirit. If you have ever heard the voice of the Holy Spirit—the "still small voice" that we talk about all the time—how did you know it was Him? How did you know it was not just your own thoughts, or some other voice?

We discern the spiritual realm with our Mind. This is a conundrum for the Mind that likes to be in control, because logic and reason prefer the *tangible*, and the spiritual realm is *intangible*. For the Mind that is used to shutting down any argument based on logic and reason, logically reasoning away the intangible is a skill at which it becomes particularly adept. This can be referred to as "a spirit of mind control," or "stubbornness of mind," or even "hard-headedness."

In the Old Testament, God referred to the Israelites as a "stiff-necked people." All of these terms encompass the idea that we have some very deeply ingrained thought pathways that need to be renewed, requiring more than just a change of thinking or behavior to overcome. "A *spirit* (or perhaps it is easier to think of it as an *attitude*) of mind-control," also alludes to the idea that it is not just our own stubbornness or hard-headedness that keeps us locked into the logical, rational thought processes that disable us from accepting things by faith. The spirit, or attitude, of Mind control is thought of as an outside spiritual influence that partners with our stubbornness or hard-headedness to keep us bound.

Ironically, to accept this "illogical and irrational" truth, one must be able to recognize the intangible existence of the spirit realm, which is a near impossibility for the Mind that likes to remain in control. The idea of a *spirit* of mind-control is easily dismissed as illogical, and we default to the same rational rhetoric that excuses our stubborn thought pathways, allowing us to continue in a logical, rational manner, while still bound by what we can readily understand and comprehend. There is no growth inside of our own comprehension! Growth requires that we be willing to step outside of what we already know so that we might grab hold of what we do not yet understand. We must take a step of faith *first*, which is then followed by understanding, not the other way around.

The Voices in our Heads…

In learning to identify the "voices" that the Mind can discern, it surprised me that God's voice is not the only voice that was familiar inside my head. Not only did I hear and know the voice of the Holy Spirit, but I was also disturbingly familiar with the voice of the enemy.

I don't mean that Satan speaks specifically to me. I'm really not that important to be singled out of 6 billion people, and he is not omnipresent; it's more akin to faulty ideas, paradigms, and worldviews that are imposed upon me from the moment I entered this world, which subtly become the "truth" upon which I build everything else. In Ephesians 6:11, Paul tells us to *"put on the full armor of God so that you can stand firm against the tactics of the devil." (HCSB).* "What are the tactics of the devil?", you may be asking. Jesus tells us exactly what the enemy came to do— *"A thief comes only to steal, kill and destroy…" (John 10:10, HCSB)*; and Peter reiterates the sentiment in 1 Peter 5:8, *"Be serious! Be alert! Your adversary, the devil, is prowling around like a roaring lion, looking for anyone he can devour" (HCSB).* The enemy's self-appointed mandate is to destroy anything that God said was good, and to tear down anyone who would seek to follow Christ. Of course, we know that he will not succeed in this mandate but, still, we are told to remain alert and stand firm. We cannot hope to do that unless we can distinguish his voice when he speaks, and learn to tune him out.

The enemy's voice, like God's voice, speaks to us, but this one is negative and destructive. This voice says things like, *"You are* a terrible father;" *"You'll always* struggle with that thing and *God will never love you* for doing that!" These statements may *sound* logical and may even *feel* true. So how do you learn to tell the difference?

The Holy Spirit is *always* speaking to us—that still, small voice that we know we are supposed to know but, most of the time, are afraid we do *not* know. The problem is, that if we spend time cultivating the wrong thoughts, we tune into the wrong frequency, drowning out the one voice we ought to be listening to.

When the Holy Spirit speaks, He speaks directly to us. He says things like, *"You are* mine. *You are* redeemed. *You are* My child and I love you!" When He must bring correction, He is gentle and encouraging and specific about what He requires of us. *"I love you* no matter what you've done—let's work on that thing together!"

Once you really get to know Him, it's hard to *not* recognize His voice when He speaks. Romans 8:16 says, *"The Spirit Himself testifies together with our spirit that we are God's children, and if children, also heirs—heirs of God and coheirs with Christ"* (HCSB). John 16:13-15 records these words of Jesus, *"When the Spirit of Truth comes, He will guide you into all the truth. For He will not speak on His own, but He will speak whatever He hears. He will also declare to you what is to come. He will glorify Me, because He will take from what is Mine and declare it to you. Everything the Father has is Mine. That is why I told you that He takes from what is Mine and will declare it to you"* (HCSB).

The voice of the Holy Spirit will bear the same characteristics and hallmarks that Paul describes in Galatians 5:22, *"But the fruit of the Spirit is love, joy, peace, patience, kindness, goodness, faith, gentleness, self-control. Against such things, there is no law"* (HCSB). Everything the Holy Spirit says will urge us toward the cultivation of such fruit in our life. His is the voice of *love*, and it is right, and good that we learn to recognize it quickly and easily.

The last voice that all of us are familiar with is the voice of our own thoughts. Something I was surprised to learn was that many of my own thoughts about myself *do not originate with me.* What do I mean by that? Our thoughts about ourselves will either agree with what God says about us, or with what the enemy wants us to believe about ourselves. The voice of our own thoughts is exemplified by first person language. "*I am* a bad father. *I can never* expect anything else. *I will always* be this way. *I am* a loser." These are our own thoughts that agree with what the enemy says about us.

"*I am* a conqueror and co-heir with Christ! *I can* do all things through Christ who strengthens me! *I have* enough faith for this!" These are our own thoughts that agree with what God says about us.

Practice Makes Perfect!

Learning to know that you know that you *know* you hear His voice is something that must be practiced—deliberately and consciously practiced—daily. In the beginning of my journey, I was a little hesitant to do the work that learning and practicing required, because I did not want to cultivate legalistic or obsessive-compulsive behaviors. If you were to eavesdrop in on the conversations I had with the Lord about this, you would have heard something like this:

Journal Entry, 4th December, 2003: "…*Some things are my choice, right? Like whether I have toast or cereal for breakfast, or what color socks I choose to put on. I don't want to become so fanatically dependent that I can't make a decision without praying on every little detail.'*

"WHY NOT?"

"*I don't want to have to pray for ten minutes over little decisions that don't take any time to make…*"

"AGAIN, WHY IS THAT A BAD THING?"

"*I don't want to get so wrapped up in making sure I do the right thing*

for You that I actually miss the thing You have for me to do!"
"BUT HOW WILL YOU KNOW WHAT I HAVE FOR YOU IF YOU DON'T KNOW HOW TO HEAR MY VOICE?"
"Well then I guess I'd have to learn how to hear from You."
"AND HOW WILL YOU DO THAT?'
"Practice?"
"HOW WILL YOU PRACTICE?"
"By listening to Your answers on all the little things…"
"DON'T WORRY, IT WON'T STAY THAT WAY. AS YOU GROW, AS YOU LEARN TO DISCERN MY VOICE, YOU WON'T HAVE TO PRAY FOR HOURS TO KNOW WHAT I WANT. YOU MAY HAVE TO REVISIT THE PROCESS—FREQUENTLY—BUT YOU NEED TO BE SATURATED IN ME TO KNOW ME…"

To be candid, I was concerned that I would become one of those fanatical Christians who couldn't function without asking God about every little move I made; it seemed quite impractical and very awkward to me, at the time. I didn't understand what would motivate someone to become so dependent on someone or something outside of themselves. To me, it looked as if they were switching off their brain to mindlessly follow some weird inner voice that may or may not be God. Well, guess what…

I get it now. I am not switching off my brain. I am not *mindlessly* following anyone. I am using my Mind to discern which voice I am listening to and changing my course, accordingly. As soon as I realize I am listening to the wrong voice, or agreeing with the wrong logic, I can quickly repent and change the way I think and tune into the voice of the Lord again.

Learning to know that you know that you know the voice of the Lord, takes effort on our part. The truth is you can't really be sure unless you spend regular time with Him. My husband, Mark, tells a great story that illustrates this point beautifully. In a conversation he had one day with a gentleman who strongly disagreed that God spoke to *anyone*,

Mark posed these two hypothetical questions:

"Suppose you met a young lady, had a half-hour conversation with her six months ago, but then did not speak with her again from that day to this. If that young lady were to walk into this crowded room, talking and laughing with her friends, would you know that she had entered the room?" The man answered correctly that no, he wouldn't be able to tell if the young lady had entered the room.

Mark asked the second hypothetical question: "Suppose you met the same young lady six months ago, had a half hour conversation with her and then continued having half hour conversations with her every day from that day to this one. If that young lady were to walk into this crowded room, talking and laughing with her friends, would you know now that she has entered the room?" The man answered that yes, he would know it.

"How would you know?" Mark asked.

The gentleman replied, "Because I'd know what she sounded like!"

Sadly, this was true of me. I wasn't spending any time reading the Word of God or interacting with the *words* of God—so I really had no hope of *knowing* what He sounded like. To be certain of the voice that I wanted to be hearing, I recognized that I had to be intentional and diligent about reading the Bible.

The more time I spent in the Word, the more familiar I became with the inflections and tones of His voice. I grew familiar with the *sorts* of things God says, and the sorts of things He would *never* say. I grew familiar with His nature and His character—that He is *good*, all the time. He is loving, and only ever says or does things for the purpose of turning our hearts back to Himself.

I grew familiar with the *weight* that came with His voice. There is a solidness, and a *rightness*, and a substance to the tone of His voice that is lacking when I listen to my own thoughts or the voice of the enemy.

Once I could easily recognize what God sounded like, practicing the incidental things, such as what to eat for breakfast or what color socks to wear, became a fine-tuning exercise that engaged my Mind further in the process of learning to hear His voice.

My husband, Mark, went on to describe something known as the S.O.A.P. tool to the young man who was certain that nobody could hear the voice of God. The tool is a good, practical, easily implemented method that will help you develop the habit of being in the Word regularly, assisting you in becoming familiar with the voice of God. You can read more about this tool in his book, "Think Speak Live. Business from Heaven's Perspective."

It's a Process…

For most of us, practicing discerning the voices we hear in our head has not been a top priority, at least for a good chunk of our lives. That's partly because it seems illogical to us to bother God with questions like "What color socks should I wear today?" We think He's probably not interested and, anyway, God wants us to think for ourselves, doesn't He?

Partly, it's also because our logical, rational Mind can easily dismiss those thoughts or voices as mere self-talk. When we reduce the voices we hear to being just "our own (sometimes neurotic) thoughts," we disallow the possibility that God might be trying to get our attention. *So what* if I wear red or green socks today? What does it matter? In the grand scheme of things, it most likely doesn't, *unless* God is asking you to practice hearing His voice among the cacophony of others that compete for your attention (or perhaps He has arranged a divine meeting for you, where someone is looking for a person wearing a red *and* a green sock to speak to them about salvation…Stranger things have happened).

Psychology, as I have understood it at a very basic level, explains those thoughts as positive and negative self-talk, which is partly true. *Your* thoughts—the ones that start with "*I am*" or "*I feel*"—as I have mentioned, will always agree with either the enemy, or with God. Positive and negative self-talk, however, starts and stops with *your own thoughts*; it doesn't consider *what God says* about you. Let me explain further.

I can change my self-talk from "I am a bad mother" to "I am a good mother." Saying it doesn't make it true. I can tell myself until I'm blue in the face that I am a good mother, but it will remain untrue until I start to *believe* it. Once I believe it, I can then start to change the behavior that goes along with the belief. If I don't believe my own self-talk, I can *think* positively about myself but still *behave* negatively— "I am a good mother," who still yells at her kids and has mistaken beliefs about her identity. The enemy can use positive self-talk in this way to keep us stuck in faulty belief cycles and destructive behaviors, just as easily as he can use negative self-talk to the same end.

When we allow the voice of the Holy Spirit to speak, He will say things like "You are an exceptional mother! Now let's work on how to stop yelling at the kids. There are better ways to get their cooperation." Alternatively, "Yes, you messed up today—but My mercies are new every morning, so you get another chance tomorrow! Let me show you an easier way..."

The enemy says things like "You're a great mother! You don't need to change a thing. They just don't appreciate you. Those kids really just need to learn some respect..." You see, the enemy would have me believe I am the world's best mother, and might even offer some behavioral changes that will make a short-term difference, like breathing techniques, counting techniques, and vocal techniques, but the first time I mess up, he's also the first to condemn me for it. "You might *think* you're a good mother, but you'll never get it right. You'll always default to messing it up!"

What God says about us is different. *What God says about us is always true*, whether we believe it or not. We can *hear* the voice of the Holy Spirit, but still *agree* with what the enemy says about us. When this happens, our thoughts about ourselves will always line up with the enemy's assessment of us.

I know we looked at this verse earlier, but bear with me a moment. Ephesians 6:11 says, *"Put on the full armor of God so that you can stand against the tactics [schemes, or tricks] of the devil."* (HCSB, extra brackets mine). In that passage, Paul goes on to tell us to put on the *"helmet of salvation."* A helmet protects the head, or for our discussion, *the Mind*, from the tactics, schemes or tricks of the enemy. The tricks and schemes of the enemy are anything that stops us from growing in our relationship with God.

As we discussed earlier, the enemy came to steal, kill, and destroy (see John 10:10), so he is intent on making sure we do not grow, even using logic and reason to keep us from the abundant life that Jesus came to give us. Salvation is ours through Jesus Christ and cannot be taken away by anyone; but if the enemy can make us *think* or *believe* that it can be, then he has us right where he wants us—stuck in condemnation, paralyzed by fear, ineffective, and stunted in our spiritual growth.

Conviction vs. Condemnation

At this point, it would be helpful to take a closer look at *conviction* and *condemnation*. Before we can discern the voices of the different members of our Boardroom, we must be keenly familiar with the voice of the Holy Spirit CEO. In this manner, we can know for certain that we are submitting ourselves to the right authority. Let's delve a little deeper into that passage from Ephesians chapter 6.

Paul tells the believers in Ephesus to *"put on the full armor of God so that **you can stand against the tactics of the devil.**"* Why? Because *"… our battle is not against flesh and blood, but against the rulers, against the authorities, against the world powers of this darkness, against the spiritual forces of evil in the heaven's."* (Ephesians 6:11&12, HCSB, emphasis mine).

One of those tactics, or 'authorities' that the enemy uses, is *condemnation*. The enemy uses condemnation to paralyze and disempower us in the battle. Condemnation is oppressively heavy, generalized, and non-specific; it causes confusion and hopelessness in our decision-making; it feels vague and is sneaky and underhanded, and it is how the enemy takes ground in our hearts. Condemnation brings with it a sense of discouragement that keeps us stuck and unable to process or move forward, even if the circumstances don't require such harsh self-judgment.

Condemnation will always drive us *away* from relationship with God. The Bible also says *"Therefore, no condemnation now exists for those in Christ Jesus." (Romans 8:1, HCSB)*. If there is no condemnation for those of us who walk with the Lord, if God Himself has decreed that no one can condemn us, then it is safe to say that any, and all, condemnation comes not from God, but from the enemy.

The *conviction* of the Holy Spirit, on the other hand, is light; it is *very* specific, and empowering, and full of hope. The conviction of the Holy Spirit enables us to see clearly what we need to change, and how we need to change it so that we may move forward. Conviction will always be loving, encouraging, and uplifting, even if it is necessarily pointed and a little painful to hear at times.

Conviction of the Holy Spirit carries the same weight, substance and rightness with it that is familiar when God speaks, always drawing us closer into relationship with the heart of the Father, restoring us in His love.

The enemy does not want us to regain that ground! Anytime we feel the oppressive heaviness and confusion of condemnation, we can be assured it is *not* from God. Any voice that brings with it the vagueness and hopelessness of condemnation is likewise *not the voice of God*.

The Mind gets to discern which voice is speaking, and then decide which voice to agree with. The more the Mind learns to listen to the voice of the Holy Spirit CEO, the louder and more easily discernible His voice is, and the more incongruous the voice of the enemy becomes with the new thought patterns of the renewed Mind. There will be a new ease to pinpointing the source of disunity and disharmony in our thinking, because we *know* to whom we are listening.

At great risk of belaboring the point—it is the Mind's job to pick the difference between the voice of our Holy Spirit CEO, (which brings conviction) and the voice of the enemy, (which brings condemnation). When you learn to recognize the difference between the two, you will be amazed at how often you *don't* get stuck!

When your Mind is renewed to remember that there is **no condemnation** for those in Christ Jesus, (as just seen in Romans 8:1), then you can identify the voice of the enemy when he speaks, and turn away from what he says and follow instead what God says—this is what repentance looks like. The job of the Holy Spirit CEO is to bring conviction, and to lead us into all truth (see again John 16:5-15).

How it Works...

Okay—now that we have some of the theory out of the way, let's get down to some practical work. At this juncture, I would like to invite you to practice hearing God with your Mind. If your Mind is particularly logical and rational, then this exercise may be a little difficult for you. Don't worry—it will get easier the more you do it. You may find it helpful to make a deal with your Mind—to do the exercise now, by faith, and to go back and analyze the outcome later. Remember, the Mind likes to be in control, and this exercise requires that it hand control over to Holy Spirit CEO. This can be a tough thing for the unregenerate Mind to do.

Record your conversation in your journal for future reference. As you work through the exercise, pay attention to any pictures you might see or the specific language used by you or by Holy Spirit CEO, as these can give you clues or reference points to pursue the conversation further. If you keep drawing a blank, ask Him why? "Lord, why can't I see? Why can't I hear?" Remember, He wants to speak more than you want to listen; often, you *will* hear or see an answer to a different question.

When I write about "seeing a picture," it's nothing weird or crazy like residual hallucinations from your LSD days; it's more of a mental picture that is common to anyone. For example: If I asked you to close your eyes and imagine your kitchen, or your bedroom at home, chances are that you would be able to call up a mental "picture" of that room in your head. If I asked you to point to where the refrigerator was and where you keep your coffee mugs, you would know exactly where to look. You would "see" all those things in your head.

Some people "see" more vividly than others, so some of you will "see" what the Lord is showing you more like a dream sequence—it will feel more real. Other's might "see" what can be referred to as "an open vision"—where you "see" what He is showing you superimposed over, or almost blocking out your natural vision.

Through whatever manner you "see," when you ask the Lord to show you something, He will do it immediately. You won't have to "build" the picture in your head; it will be there instantly, and in great detail. You might see one thing, like an object that is highlighted in surrounding darkness, or you might see a whole room or scene laid out before you. Whatever it is, it will usually surprise you because it does not come from you.

If you see something disturbing that freaks you out, don't abandon the exercise. Sometimes the enemy's thoughts, that we have spent a lifetime agreeing with, will want to assert themselves. That is why it is extremely important to ask the Holy Spirit CEO to journey with you through these exercises. You can ask Him to explain, destroy, or illuminate to you what is happening—however He directs you and whatever seems appropriate.

If you still can't get beyond the freaky stuff, ask a different question. Ask Him "Do you love me?", "How much do you love me?", "Will you ever leave me?", "Will you come with me on this journey?" Then, "Where do *You* want me to start?" Record your answers, and go where He leads you.

For those of you who are having a particularly hard time agreeing with the theology of this exercise, and there's bound to be someone, spend a few moments thinking on these scriptures:

Matthew 7:7-11, "Keep asking, and it will be given to you. Keep searching, and you will find. Keep knocking, and the door will be opened to you. For everyone who asks, receives, and the one who searches, finds, and to the one who knocks, the door will be opened. What man among you, if his son asks for bread, will give him a stone? Or if he asks for a fish, will give him a snake? If you, then, who are evil, know how to give good gifts to your children, **how much more will your Father in heaven give good things to those who ask Him!**" *(HCSB, emphasis mine).*

Proverbs 25:2, "It is the Glory of God to conceal a matter, and the glory of kings to investigate a matter" (HCSB).

Jeremiah 29:13, "You will seek me and find me when you search for me with all your heart" (HCSB).

Isaiah 26:3, "You will keep the mind that is dependent on You in perfect peace, for it is trusting in You" (HCSB).

The first exercise for you is to trust that if you ask the Lord to show you a picture, then the Lord is going to show you a picture. He wants to talk with you, communicate with you, and interact with you, so much more than you want to hear from Him. Trust that He will do the good thing you have asked of Him!

Now it's Your Turn

Get yourself comfortable, in an undisturbed time and space, and close your eyes. Thank God for His presence with you. Praise Him for His greatness, and His grace. Then, ask Him, "Holy Spirit, I ask that you lead me into all truth, as it was promised that You would. Would You talk to me, or show me now, how do *You* see my Mind?"

Once you have your picture—visually or in words—record what you heard and saw. This is the beginning point for your dialogue with Holy Spirit CEO. Ask Him about the things you don't understand. Ask Him to comment on the things He is revealing to you. Tell Him how you feel, seeing and hearing these things.

Ask Him what He likes about your Mind, and what He wants to work on with you to change. Is there anything that He has shown you that you need to renew your thinking on, in particular? Is there anything for which you need to confess or repent? Is there anything else He wants to show you or talk to you about in this session? Keep going until He says "Enough." Finish your session in whatever manner you feel is appropriate—more praise and worship, thanksgiving, or just hanging with Him in silence for a while.

At a later date, remember the deal you made with your Mind? Read over the account of your time with the Lord with fresh eyes. Are there any other questions that come up for you? As you read, your Mind will be working overtime. There will be things that ring true for you and other things that you might disagree with. What voice is the Mind discerning, on each of those points? Which voice agrees and which disagrees with what you have recorded?

I encourage you to go digging through scripture to validate or discount the things you experienced. The Holy Spirit CEO will *never* contradict the Word of God, so anything that goes against scripture can be easily dismissed as *not God*! You might be surprised at how the Lord spoke to you—in a seemingly unbiblical way that lines up solidly with

Biblical concepts—He's just that creative!

This will not be the end of your conversation. As is the case with any close friend, you will find that you will come back to a particular topic over and over, even when there are other topics on the table for discussion. If this is done in a single session, great; if not, all the better.

---
chapter three

THE HEART

"I will give you a new heart and put a new spirit within you; I will remove your heart of stone and give you a heart of flesh…"
(Ezekiel 36:26, HCSB).

Journal Entry, sometime in September, 2003: *"I can't help but think that my Heart will need a lot of work…because if I am honest with myself, sometimes I allow my rebellious pride to indulge in whatever wanderings and flights of fancy appeal to it at the time. Getting lost in a good story is the ultimate in escapism for me, and like a choice between health food and junk food, some of what I choose to indulge in is not so good for me in large volumes! So—what does my Heart look like? I'm almost too scared to know.*

"The silhouette is perfect—perfect shape, size, position; pulsing regularly with life—but it's just a dark shape, no color, and I cannot see the textures or contours of its surface. This is what people see—a neat little package (seemingly), all in order. Then the light shifts, to spotlight it from the front.

"My Heart is not overweight, but it's very flabby, pale, and tired looking—like someone trying to give the illusion of a trim figure by holding their tummy in and puffing their chest out…it is just so worn out by trying to look it's best and appearing to be in perfect shape that everything

*else has been neglected (that is: all the other things that **would** keep it in shape). My heart indulges in things that might make it feel better in the moment, but not keep it in shape..."*

This took me a little while, but I realized, at some point, that I had not asked for Jesus' perspective of what I had seen. I finally got around to asking Him...

Journal Entry, 20th October, 2003: *"How do You see my Heart, Lord?"*
"YOU'VE ONLY LOOKED AT YOUR HEART FROM THE FRONT. WALK AROUND. LOOK BEHIND. WHAT DO YOU SEE?"
"I see a life support system complete with wires, alarms, tubes...Each one has its function in keeping the Heart going, but most (if not all) are unnecessary. My Heart can't move because of all the things I'm attached to; it's connected to...I don't know what; all these wires and tubes and alarms and paraphernalia correspond directly with all the objects and people walking around in my boardroom, don't they? Each one represents someone or something that I am letting have too much input into my Heart/life.

Me, trying to read Your Word, is like trying to breathe on my own but the breathing tube is still in my throat and I'm gagging on it. Rather than wanting to remove it, I'm just not fighting—I'm giving up and letting the breathing tube breathe for me...

This represents, more than anything, my dependence on fiction to relax. I watch a lot of television, which isn't shocking in itself, but it stays unchallenged and unanswered by Bible reading, prayer, worship and meditation. Maybe the problem isn't so much that I watch television, but that I am so unbalanced by it."

The second board member I want to introduce to you is the Heart. You may have heard, or used, such terms as, "He is so hard-hearted!", "I don't have the heart for this...", "I wear my heart on my sleeve", or "She has such a big heart!" These sayings refer to a person's character, or the thing or things that they are known for to us.

The Heart is referred to, in the Bible, as being "the well-spring" or the "source" of life (Proverbs 4:23). In the Old Testament, the word "heart" is used to describe both the physical organ, as well as the whole being, the governing center of all the responses of our life. The Hebrew text translates Proverbs 4:23, ***"With all diligence, keep your heart,*** *for out of it are the issues of life" (The Interlinear Bible, emphasis mine).*

The word "heart" in the New Testament is used in a similar way, meaning our "inner man". The Greek text translates Luke 6:45 *"The good man, out of the good treasure of the heart of him, brings forth the good; and the evil man, out of the evil treasure of the heart of him, brings forth the evil.* ***For out of the abundance of the heart speaks the mouth of him****"(The Interlinear Bible, emphasis mine).*

All issues and essential motivations of our life are found in the Heart. The Heart harbors its own judgments, expectations, and way of looking at things—so we actually do live out of what is in our Heart. We keep our secret hopes, longings, desires, and dreams in our Heart. If we allow these secret cravings to rule in our Heart, they become what the Bible defines as "idols." Ezekiel 14:3 says, *"Son of man, these men have set **up idols in their hearts** and have put sinful stumbling blocks before their faces. Should I be consulted by them at all?"(HCSB, emphasis mine).*

WHAT DO YOU TREASURE?

The Heart can be thought of like a mansion, a storehouse, or a treasure house with many rooms where we store every experience we have had in our lives, as well as the various things we value, worship and feed on for life. Some of these rooms we know about, but most of them are hidden from our awareness, in our unconscious or sub-conscious.

Jesus tells us in Matt 6:19-21 *"Don't collect for yourselves treasures on earth, where moth and rust destroy and where thieves break in and steal. But collect for yourselves treasures in Heaven, where neither moth nor rust destroys, and where thieves don't break in and steal.* **For where your treasure is, there your heart will be also.**" *(HCSB, emphasis mine).*

In a spiritual sense, the things we treasure or store in our Heart are also stored in heaven. Therefore, it is important not to treasure or place value on the wrong things. Paul warns the church in Corinth of this when he says: *"According to God's grace that was given to me, I have laid a foundation as a skilled master builder, and another builds on it. But each one must be careful how he builds on it.... If any one builds on that foundation with gold, silver, costly stones, wood, hay, or straw, each one's work will become obvious, for the day will disclose it, because it will be revealed by fire; the fire will test the quality of each one's work. If any one's work that he has built survives, he will receive a reward. If any one's work is burned up, it will be lost, but he will be saved; yet it will be like an escape through fire"* (1Corinthians 3:10-17, HCSB).

Storing treasures in heaven, and what we build on the foundation of Jesus Christ, are one and the same. The things we build with silver, gold and costly stones equate to treasures worthy of being stored in heaven, because they will survive the fire, or the testing. The things we build with wood, hay and straw equate to treasures on earth that can be destroyed or corrupted; these things will not survive the fire of testing. Basically, what Jesus is saying in Matthew chapter six and what Paul is saying in 1 Corinthians chapter three is this: *How you think, speak, and live on earth matters in Heaven!* All of it is connected.

Several years ago, MasterCard began an ad campaign that went something (a bit) like this: You see a wide angled shot of a couple on a motorcycle, riding through the autumn leaves in the late afternoon sun. The voice over speaks. "Hiring a Harley Davidson for the weekend, two thousand, five hundred dollars." The camera zooms in closer. "New leather jacket, one thousand, four hundred dollars." The camera zooms in closer again, showing the smiling couple's perfectly white teeth as they laugh and enjoy the scenery. "First weekend without the kids in ten years…Priceless!" Well, maybe there wasn't one *exactly* like that, but there *could've* been one similar.

The ad campaign has been running for about nine years, producing approximately one hundred and sixty ads over that timeframe. The success of this ad campaign was in the "priceless" tagline. "Priceless" means that you can't put a price tag on it; that the worth of the thing is far beyond anything money can buy. You can look at all the trappings and the bling in the ad and miss the thing that is truly priceless—the thing that can't be bought. This ad campaign called our attention to the "insignificant" things in life, and made us think a little harder about what we considered to be "priceless" in our own lives.

When it comes to storing treasures in heaven, it's easy to get distracted with the trappings and the bling of "doing good." Helping every year at the homeless shelter at Christmas or Thanksgiving because it looks good on your resume will cost you. You will gain a certain measure of reward for standing in the cold ladling soup to strangers for three hours. Ivy league schools take notice of community service hours; but if your Heart is not in it, that's all the reward you'll get. "Handing a cup of hot soup to the least of these, with a smile and a hug…? Priceless!" Your reward in heaven will be far beyond anything money can buy.

Let's look at it this way. We know that the Kingdom of God is opposite to what we think it should be. This is made evident every time Jesus shares a parable; the Prodigal Son, the Lost Sheep, The Lost Coin, and the Good Samaritan, to name but a few. The Beatitudes and the rest of the Sermon on the Mount, as recorded in Matthew, are full of what the world would see as contradictions—turn the other cheek, love your enemy, pray for those who persecute you…all these admonitions are backwards. Jesus' own ministry exemplified His servant heart toward people, and He demonstrated this dramatically when He knelt to wash the disciples' feet at the last supper.

This backward approach to the Kingdom of God is further demonstrated in Matthew 10:39: *"Anyone finding his life will lose it, and anyone losing his life because of Me will find it"* (HCSB). Again—in Mark 9:35, when Jesus asked His disciples what they were arguing about, and had received a shameful non-answer from them because then they would have to admit that they were arguing about who would be the greatest—He sat them down and taught them, *"If anyone wants to be first, he must be last of all and servant of all"* (HCSB).

There are so many passages in the Gospels alone that speak of this, but perhaps my favorite is the parable of the Sheep and the Goats, in Matthew 25:31 and following. There is no better description, for me, of how our service to others, in the name of Jesus, touches His heart. *"Whatever you did for one of the least of these brothers of mine, you did for Me"* (HCSB). Oh I want to be known in Heaven as one who served Jesus well!

Bearing all of this in mind, the question, "What do you treasure?" suddenly brings with it a whole new weight of realization as we consider the heavenly value of some of the things on which we spend our time, effort, and money. While it is true that we all treasure different things, everything that each person treasures can be categorized in similar ways. Every person on earth has what we would call "core values"—those things that define the way that we think and govern our approach to life; but not all people share the same core values.

For instance, I might place a high value on praying before I eat, but the person sitting at the table across from me in the food court at the mall might consider that to be old-fashioned and superstitious.

The term "relativism" comes to mind here. I am not talking about "what feels right for me is right for me, and what feels right for you is right for you..." I'm talking about the things we value that are shaped by our culture, our family, social norms, and affinity groups. Our core values do not give us license to do or say whatever we want; but what we store and file away in our Heart defines our own personal matrix— or set of standards—of how to behave in the world.

Saying grace before eating a meal is a value shared by thousands, if not millions of other people around the world. The motivating force behind *why* I say grace, however, can be very different for me than for someone else. For me, saying grace before a meal—or "blessing the food", or "giving thanks," whatever name you choose to give it—is not just a cozy family tradition. Rather, it is born from thankfulness at the core of my being that God would provide nourishment for my physical Body. I also offer thanks for the food because my parents taught me that it was the right and proper thing to do.

How different would my motivation be if I had been taught that to *not* be thankful and bless what I ate before I ate it would incur God's wrath and anger in the form of malnourishment and food poisoning? If the motivation behind my thankfulness is fear, how thankful am I, really? We can draw comfort from what we believe is right, but comfort does not guarantee "right."

So, if our Heart is like a storehouse with many rooms, and everything we have ever experienced has been stored, or filed away, in those rooms, what exactly does that mean? Because we all filter our experiences differently, and each person treasures different things and holds different core values, we will store and categorize those experiences in different ways. This means that two people can be present for the exact same event, but each will process and store that event as two very different experiences.

It's All a Matter of Perspective…

When I was little, I had an overwhelming fear of spiders. Not much has changed now that I am grown—I am still not very fond of spiders. I recall a time in my childhood when I was playing in the cubby house that my Pa had built for my brothers and me in our backyard.

This cubby house was awesome—it had two levels inside and two rooftop levels outside, and a fireman's pole from the top level down to the ground. I loved the cubby house because inside, I could play "house"—I had a kitchen area, a bedroom area, and a place to store all my dress-up costumes; my brothers liked it for a completely different reason. They could climb all over the outside of it and play war games and forts and chase each other all up and down the ladders and fireman's pole. For three young kids, it was a dream playhouse…until I discovered that my dress up box was a favorite hiding pace for spiders.

Unless you have ever lived in Australia and are familiar with the giant huntsman spiders that reside there, you might not appreciate my intense dislike for these hairy creatures. Google them—I dare you to not be grossed out. So, I pulled out some fairy-princess creation that poorly reflected the grandness of my imagination, and as I lifted it out of the box, my eye caught an accessory I hadn't embellished this particular outfit with.

The spider sat with its horrendous hairy legs spread over the bodice of my gown—right where a sparkly, jeweled brooch would have looked its most dazzling best—and I let out a scream and instantly dropped the dress at my feet. Not a smart move, because now the dress, with its ghastly inhabitant, was between me and the door, so there was no escape. I was trapped, and paralyzed with fear!

My brothers, hearing the commotion, came running to see what had caused my distress, as did my Pa, who happened to be working in the garden. When my brothers saw me standing in the corner with no apparent reason for my screaming, they did what any self-respecting brother would do. Shrugged it off and turned to go back to their game. Pa came in behind them before they could leave, though, and in that moment, I managed to squeak out the single word, "Spider!"

"Cool! Where is it?" This from my brothers, who, in spite of their brave words, took a few steps back and looked nervously around before settling into a position near the door—far enough away to escape should the need arise, but close enough to see the hideous occupant of the dress. I stood, shaking like a leaf in the wind, pointing to the dress at my feet.

Pa stepped into the cubby and picked up the dress at the shoulders. The spider was no longer present on the bodice; my relief was short lived, however, because a new scream found its way past my lips as I spotted it crawling down the length of the skirt towards Pa's work boots.

"This little thing?" Pa's smile was *not* reassuring. Neither was his next move. He reached down and plucked the spider off the dress. Now it sat (probably stunned) in the palm of his hand. I think I might have wet myself, just a little bit.

As I recall, my brothers gathered closer to see, and Pa—just to prove how very harmless these creatures really were—tickled the spider's butt just enough to get it moving, and it began to crawl. He undid the button on the sleeve of his shirt, and I watched, horrified, as it disappeared up his sleeve. My brothers watched, probably equally as horrified, but in a completely different and fascinated way. The spider came out at the top of Pa's collar, and he scooped it up to show us, up close. I cowered in the corner. My brothers—still a respectfully safe distance away—leaned in for a closer look.

"Do you want to touch it?"

"No thanks!" All three of us chorused. Pa let the spider go outside, somewhere far away from the cubby house.

"That was so cool!" one of my brothers shouted.

"Yeah—cool!" agreed the other. Then they went back to their game. Pa went back to the garden. I shuddered as I stayed behind.

"That was gross!" I said as I picked up the dress and stuffed it back into the dress up box and decided that Mum probably needed my help inside. Weeks would pass before I could go back into that cubby house to play.

I'm not convinced that my brothers were any less wary of spiders than I; but that event was experienced differently by all three of us, differently again by Pa; and again, most likely quite differently by the spider…not that I really cared at the time *what* the spider thought.

From my perspective, it was traumatic enough to prevent me from venturing near the cubby house again for quite some time. From my brothers' perspective, it was just a cool thing to witness in the middle of their game. From Pa's perspective, it was an opportunity to teach us about spiders. Three different perspectives and three different experiences surrounding the same event.

You see, whether an event is traumatic or not depends on a person's perspective. Perspective is determined by how a person thinks. Everything that happens to us is processed, or filtered through our Mind, and stored in the Heart. As each new experience is stored in the Heart, it is placed into a room, and categorized, according to similar experiences. A traumatic experience is often thrown into a room and locked in, and left there…sometimes for years. We tend to not want to relive traumatic experiences so we are more than happy to leave them there, untouched, and unprocessed.

So, these events and experiences are stored in our Heart. Then what? Well, when we find ourselves in a similar situation or circumstance, the Heart sends a message to the Mind in the form of an Emotion. That Emotion might be fear, sadness, inappropriate humor, or anger—whatever was attached to the memory of the original event. The Emotion lets the Mind know that there is something already in the Heart that relates to the current circumstance.

If the Mind does not know how to interpret these messages from the Heart, it will dismiss the message as an illogical response and shut the Emotion down. This causes a compounding effect on the Heart, and adds current trauma to past trauma. If you've ever heard the term "to rub salt in the wound", this would be a perfect example.

Let's think of it another way. If the Heart's job is to record everything that happens in our life, and keep the records for the use and edification of the members of the boardroom, and then those members dismiss this job as meaningless or illogical and unnecessary, how might the Heart respond? By becoming resentful that it is not heard. By becoming belligerent in the manner in which it relates to the other board members. Perhaps it will become passive-aggressive, appearing to give up, but sending Emotional messages for the slightest and tiniest of situations.

We will talk more on the Emotions in the next chapter, but out of control Emotions are essentially a Heart issue. If the Heart is not heard, it will manipulate to be obeyed; and if it can't win that either, it will team up with other board members to bring about the destruction of the member that is in control. This is what makes the Heart a CEO wanna-be. If it can't be heard, it must rule, and if it can't rule, then it will make life extremely difficult for the one who does rule.

Now before you fall into a hopeless heap because there is *no way* you can sort through all the stuff that's stored in your Heart, be encouraged. God does not expect you to go digging through all the rooms of your Heart to find and sort out every thing that was stored in there. Susanne Fengler would say often, "Only work on as much or as little as what the Lord tells you to do." These are wise words of advice that will keep you from getting bogged down and depressed by the mountain of stuff we all have.

Learning to hear what your Heart is saying; learning to hear the messages it sends; and learning to hear the voice of the Lord are the keys to discerning what needs to be done and what does not. We touched on this in the last chapter—it is the Mind's job to discern which voice is speaking. If the Mind discerns correctly, the Heart can process more accurately and store the information appropriately. If the Mind discerns incorrectly or applies a faulty filter to the information as it comes through to the Heart, the Heart will either be unable to process, or will process inaccurately, which can then lead to trauma.

Whenever the Heart stores a traumatic event, it stores a very strong memory of the emotional response, along with the trauma; it's as if a piece of you stops maturing at the point of the trauma, and the Heart stores that piece of you in the room with it.

This becomes evident when you find yourself in any situation that in any way resembles the trauma. We can find ourselves in reaction mode; and how often have we noticed of ourselves, and others, that in that moment we behaved like a toddler having a temper tantrum?... Or like a spoiled ten-year-old?... Or an insecure adolescent?... This is because the information, and the ensuing reactions that were stored with the event, were faulty. A traumatic event does not have to be something that was particularly violent or horrific, although those types of events certainly fall into that category.

Getting back to the spider story, why did I process the event as a trauma, while my brothers and my Pa did not? Before you ask—I know it was traumatic because my first instinct and involuntary action, to this day, when I see a *large* spider is to scream. Loudly.

Somewhere, leading up to that event, my Mind had processed away some information about spiders. Perhaps I had read something at school about tarantulas and the poisonous bird-eating monster spiders found in various regions of the world. Perhaps, as was every young Australian in my generation, I was unduly influenced by the popular song about the red-back spider on the toilet seat that was waiting to bite unsuspecting persons on the nether regions (don't ask!); it's entirely possible that I had overheard adult conversations about poisonous spider bites that were never intended for my ears. All this information was collated by my Mind and filtered into the storerooms of my Heart, so that when I had my own encounter with a spider, I was fully prepared with enough propaganda to elicit a response of fear.

I took the information I heard and interpreted a lot of it incorrectly and, therefore, believed part-truths and outright lies about spiders that influenced my reactions. I really don't know what I thought a huntsman spider could do to me—the fact is, as ugly as they are, they are harmless to humans. Unless you eat them. I think they may be poisonous if you eat them; but I digress—the point is, if I had filtered the information differently from the start, I might have processed the event differently and not have been traumatized by it.

Some events, by their very nature, are traumatic in and of themselves. These events need no previous faulty information for our Heart to categorize them as "trauma". Rape, assault, child-molestation, traumatic accidents, or war-zone situations would be some examples of these. When these types of events occur, how we are allowed or disallowed to *process* the trauma will play a big part in our recovery and healing *following* it. Long after the physical wounds have healed, our Heart can carry wounds that paralyze and disable us. Our emotional healing will depend on the information that our Heart receives *after* the event.

Two people can experience the same event; one will be traumatized and the other will not. One will see themselves as a victim; the other will rise up and be victorious. One will move on, and the other will remain "stuck" in the event. This may be related to vows that we make in the middle of the trauma in order to survive.

The Binding Nature of a Vow…

A good friend of mine, Sue Jenkins, would often say, "You know, everyone on this planet is just doing the very best they know how, just to survive." There is truth and wisdom in that. At any given point, we are just trying our best to survive—and this is true of how our Heart behaves in a traumatic situation.

When something happens to us that is out of our control, it is not uncommon for our Heart to make a vow. A vow—in the Old Testament and in the New Testament—was a binding declaration and promise. Acts 18:18 records briefly that Paul (or perhaps Aquila) had, *"…Shaved his head at Cenchreae because of a vow."* A vow can be made to perform or abstain from performing certain acts. From the *Illustrated Dictionary of the Bible* (Herbert Lockyer, Sr., Editor, pp1088): "Vow—a solemn promise or pledge that binds a person to perform a specified act or to behave in a certain manner." "All vows were made to God as a promise in expectation of His favor… or in thanksgiving for His Blessings…"

God looked upon those who did not fulfill a vow or promise as being cheats, or deceivers. In Malachi 1:14, *"**The deceiver is cursed** who has an acceptable animal in his flock and makes a vow but sacrifices a defective animal to the Lord."* (HCSB, emphasis mine).

In the spiritual realm, a vow is also binding. When our Heart makes a vow to follow Jesus, and accept the sacrifice He made on our behalf at the cross, it secures our salvation; it is a binding declaration that acknowledges the rule and reign of Jesus in our lives, and one that is heard in the spiritual realm and lived out in the physical realm. Romans 10:9 says, *"If you openly declare that Jesus is Lord **and believe in your heart** that God raised Him from the dead, you will be saved."* (NLT, emphasis mine).

In the same way, when our Heart makes a vow amid trauma, it is a binding declaration of its own rule and reign over that area of our lives. That vow is heard in the spiritual realm and lived out in the physical realm, often in ways that are detrimental to our spiritual growth and physical wellbeing.

When our Heart vows to maintain its own rule and reign over a particular area of our lives, we cut Jesus out of the picture. We deny Him access to that piece of our lives. We leave Him sitting on the sidelines. If we are to give Him authority over any given area, we need to revoke, cancel, or withdraw our Heart's claim of authority over that area. Otherwise, we will always struggle to give Him permission and power to work in those areas of our lives. We may *want* Him to have that authority, but He won't really *have* authority.

Breaking a Heart vow is as simple as repenting of the vow that was made, and remaking the vow, if you like, to reinstate His authority over that area. I say simple, but sometimes it is not *easy* to do. Relinquishing Heart a vow requires that our Heart be willing to explore the possibility that we may have been wrong in our assessment of the traumatic situation, and then be willing to accept Jesus' assessment of that situation.

To move past our faulty beliefs, we first must recognize them as being faulty. When we hold on to something and call it "truth" for long enough, it becomes very difficult to let it go just because someone somewhere said it might not be truth anymore. If the Heart is not willing, then its sway over the Will is powerful, and not much will be accomplished.

I write this carefully and with the full realization that, for some, there were traumas that came against them while they were in a position of weakness. For the child that was molested, or the young person who was cruelly beaten by a person who was older, stronger, or in any other way more powerful than them, this is a jagged pill to swallow. "What do you mean, I was wrong in my assessment of that situation? I was there! It's pretty accurate!"

The most common question I hear people ask regarding traumas such as these is, "Where was God anyway? Why didn't He stop it from happening, if He loves me so much?" One hundred percent of the time, *when that Heart is willing* to allow Jesus to show them the trauma through His eyes, the Heart receives healing and can move forward.

Why? Because during the traumatic event, the Heart is *just doing the very best it can* to make sense of the situation and *survive*. The wounded Heart will say things like "I'm all alone. There's nothing I can do to stop this. No one cares. *I will never...!*" Fill in the blank. *I will never* be bad again, then he won't beat me. *I will never* let someone push me around like that again. *I will never* again let someone get that close to me. *I will never* show my weakness like that again.

When the Heart makes declarations such as these, it will hold itself accountable to that vow from that point onward, and is essentially saying, "I will control this piece of my world. God did not step in/was unable/didn't care—I will fend for myself!" The vow is sealed in the spiritual realm because our Holy Spirit CEO hears it, and being the gentleman that He is, He allows us our right to free will. We also seal that vow if, and when, we speak the sentiment out loud, because now it has been heard and ratified in the spirit realm, and a stronghold is created. We openly declare that *we* will be lord of that area of our lives, and we believe in our Heart that we are right in our assessment of the traumatic event.

When these kinds of vows are made, the Heart will not always be cooperative in getting straight to the point and dealing with the issue. If we are not familiar with the process and the practice of listening to our Heart, we will struggle to bring it into alignment with anything that the Holy Spirit CEO desires, because the Heart in this state is quite happy being captain of its own destiny.

Learning to Work With Your Heart...

The purpose of learning to listen to our Heart is simply to allow it to be heard. Like any other person in the world, we want to be heard. We want someone, somewhere to care. How often do the phrases, "You never listen!" and, "You don't even care!" find themselves keeping company?

While it is important to always *listen* to what our Heart is saying, it is not always appropriate to *obey* what it says. The unregenerate Heart (the Heart that is *not* submitted to the Holy Spirit CEO) will posture and bluff its way into making you believe that its way is the *only* way to finding true happiness; the Heart that is fully submitted to the Holy Spirit CEO will be content just to have its say, and then support whatever He requires, because it knows that *true* happiness is found in humble obedience.

My Heart was the first board member the Lord introduced me to. Up until that point, I was uninterested and uninspired by my Bible. For all my ideals and asking God if there was more to the Christian life than *this*, I would much rather sit and watch television, or a movie, or read a good book (or a not so good book, whichever way you look at it) than take time out with God.

I *knew* that spending time with God was an essential for every good Christian, but in my Mind, it was all a bit too legalistic, and I knew well enough that God wasn't into legalism. So, my Bible stayed under my bed gathering dust, for the most part, while I continued to present myself as "spiritual" and mature.

I did what a pastor's wife should—sang in the choir and on the worship team, led Bible study groups, and went to prayer meetings…but God and I both knew I was somewhat fraudulent in my representation of my relationship with Him. Guilt set in, and with it an overwhelming fear that at some point I would be found out, and the thought of it was humiliating.

Until I was introduced to my Heart, I felt little hope that anything would ever change. I realized that my Heart, even though I could pinpoint my conversion, had never really gotten to know the Lord. This threw me into a crisis of confidence regarding my salvation—how could I *possibly* be saved if my Heart did not know Jesus?

Just as alarmingly, I came to realize that there was not much trust between my Heart and any other part of me. I had learned, over the course of my life, to shut down what my Heart was trying to tell me, because I had come to believe that I was overly emotional and too sensitive. How very freeing it was to discover that I am neither of those things!

In October of 2003, I began to work with my Heart, slowly weaning it from my addiction to fiction and teaching it to turn to the Source of Life for its sustenance and rejuvenation. I put myself on a television fast, of sorts. I cut out approximately twenty hours of television viewing per week, and resolved to spend as much of that time reading my Bible and journaling as I could.

Following a few months of very real struggle, the help and support of my husband, Mark, and with a renewed awareness of the presence of the Holy Spirit, I found I was finally able to break the cycle. I can point to that period now and categorically state that *that* is when my hunger for the Word of God was reignited. *That* is when my relationship with Him started growing and deepening and going places I never could have imagined. Suddenly, my *Heart* was in it, and once that little miracle occurred, no one could convince me to be mediocre, *ever* again.

Keeping Your Heart Engaged in the Process...

Learning how to work with your Heart is one thing; learning how to keep it engaged is another thing, entirely. Sometimes, it seems that each new incident, each new encounter requires that I reintroduce all these concepts to my Heart, all over again. While it is true that the more I work with my Heart and the more my Heart spends time with the Lord, the more it begins to trust Him and the easier this will get, it is also true that each encounter is like a clean slate.

Do you remember I mentioned that when trauma hits, a part of our Heart stops growing and maturing at that point? That's the reason why we find ourselves reacting like a spoiled teenager or a frightened six-year old. I think that this forms part of the answer to this difficulty.

Just because the Heart has worked through its stuff with the Lord one hundred times before, does not mean that it will always be one hundred per cent willing to jump into the process again the one hundred and first time—because with each new issue, it must relearn the goodness of God, and His trustworthiness.

Susanne Fengler would always have us "check in" with our Heart before we started any interaction with the Holy Spirit. Depending on the event that was being brought to Lord, the Heart's reaction could be anything from pure rebellion, all the way through to willing cooperation. For the times that the Heart is *un*willing, we need to learn the skill of working with it, identifying the roadblocks to cooperation and allowing our Heart the space it needs to get comfortable talking with the Lord. The more you spend the time doing this, the easier it will become—His voice gets easier and easier to recognize the more you hear Him. Consider the following examples: (To clarify, when my Heart speaks, I have denoted it with an "H". When the Holy Spirit CEO/Jesus speaks, it is denoted with capital letters)

Journal Entry, 3rd February, 2004: "… 'Lord, how is my Heart?'
"ASK IT…"
H: "Why do you always need Him to tell you to ask me?"
"Because you won't talk to me—but I figured that maybe you'd talk to Jesus. You withdraw when I say that. Why?"
H: "The Mind is butting in. Send it away and I'll talk."
"Lord Jesus, my Mind is too domineering; it wants to control everything; it wants the credit for solving the problems—but that credit belongs to You. Please help my Mind…"
"WHAT DO YOU WANT ME TO DO?"
"I don't know—give my Mind a rest, perhaps? To know stuff in my Heart without thinking about it first seems like a strange concept to me. I will trust that while I am working with You, You will only allow Your truth into my Heart…"

Sometimes the Mind needs to be reminded that God is good to His word, as in the above example. Sometimes, our Heart needs reassurance that it will be heard. Sometimes, the Heart is just confused and hurt and needs to get some of that junk off its chest.

Journal Entry, 17th April, 2007: "Lord—I'm sorry. I'm tired and I want to do things Your way—as long as it doesn't involve me going to that person and working it out. Please help my Heart work through this…"
"DOES YOUR HEART **WANT** TO WORK THROUGH THIS?"
"Heart, what do you think?"
H: "Depends…
"On what?"
H: "On what it is I have to do."
"Why?"
H: "I don't want to go to that person because that person hurts. That person is prickly, angry, and really well armed. I have no defense against that kind of force!"

"YOU HAVE ME."

H: "But that person claims to have You, too! How can we both have You and still be so opposite? We can't both be right...!"

Journal Entry, 8th May, 2007: H: "So I'm sitting up in bed, ignoring the phone, with this anxious knot in my stomach twisting tighter and tighter and all I want to do is go to sleep for a really long time until it all goes away. I'm eating wrong (I've overdosed on chocolate and chips again) and I just want to hide and not deal with anything. So where do I start?"

"With Jesus."

H: "I don't know if I could cope with what He might say."

"Why not give it a go?"

H: "Shouldn't I be reading the Bible or something?"

"You can, and you have been, but you haven't connected with Jesus for a while."

H: "I guess not...but I don't know what to say to Him. I don't know where to start."

"How about "Hi Jesus! How are You?"

H: "How about "Hi Jesus! **Where** are You? I haven't seen You for while"... "

"I'M HERE."

H: "So...How've You been...?"

"MISSING YOU."

H: "Really?"

"YEP. HOW'VE **YOU** BEEN?"

H: "Tired. Anxious. Fearful. I guess You heard what I said before?"

"YEAH. I HEARD..."

You can see from these interactions that the Heart is not always easy to deal with. Sometimes its attitude is really bad; it can be belligerent and disrespectful; it can also be contrite and pliable to His will. There have been many times when I have begun a conversation between my

Heart and the Lord, fully expecting to deal with a particular issue or event, but during the course of the conversation, it becomes very clear that the Lord has an entirely different agenda.

Holy Spirit CEO asks questions of my Heart that I would not have come up with on my own, and the outcome of those sessions goes way beyond anything I would have hoped for at the beginning. I think I'm sitting down to talk about one thing, but it turns out that my Heart was bound by something else entirely. Getting through the initial stages of a bad attitude to get to the point obliges one to have patience, and exercise gentleness, kindness and self-control with oneself. Who knew the fruits of the Spirit would be helpful in dealing with our *own* junk?

Now It's Your Turn...

So, now it's your turn again. Find some time to sit with the Lord and ask Him some questions about your Heart. Schedule it into your week if you must. While you are speaking with the Lord about your Heart, it is important to know that your Heart may well be quite reticent about taking part. Do not be surprised if feelings of hesitancy, fear, skepticism or rebellion come to the surface. As with the previous exercise with the Mind, our Heart might need a little coaxing to feel comfortable with the process. Our Heart can throw some astonishingly negative comments at us and be surprisingly unwilling to cooperate. If you have never really learned to listen to your Heart before, you may feel skeptical about the validity of this exercise.

Remember that your Heart needs to be heard, but not always obeyed, so reassure your Heart that you are doing this so you can learn to pay better attention to what it is constantly trying to tell you. If needed, remind the Mind of its God given task of analyzing so it does not default to its dysfunctional task of controlling.

Another thing that is helpful to remember is that you do not have to go looking for traumatic events to work on. You don't even have to go looking for *anything* to work on. If something naturally comes up, ask the Lord about it, certainly, but there is no need to dredge up past events or traumas just so you will have something to talk about. Begin the conversation, and go wherever the Lord leads you. Spending hours talking to the Lord about what He likes to do for fun, and sharing what you like to do is a perfectly valid way to make use of your time with Him; it's a "get to know you" session between your Heart and the Lord, so take the pressure off yourself to achieve anything other than learning to hang out with the Lord and talk to Him.

Begin by thanking the Lord for the gift of your Heart. Praise Him for His wisdom in providing this most precious gift to you. Ask Him if there is anything He specifically wants to tell you about your Heart. Enter into dialogue with Him. Ask for clarification; ask Him to show you a picture; ask Him what He thinks about your Heart. Don't ask a question for the sake of asking a question; ask it for the sake of beginning a conversation with Him.

Proverbs 4:23 says, *"Guard your **heart** above all else, for it is the source of life." (HCSB, emphasis mine).* Many of us have not guarded our Hearts adequately—this exercise was one that helped me to learn how to bring my Heart to Jesus and really begin to guard it the way He always intended for me to guard it.

To rewrite traumatic events and change our response to future events *is* possible, but there is no quick fix, and there are no short-cuts. We must be willing to do the work. You *can* get to a place where those traumas no longer have a hold on you, and the Heart no longer needs to send those emotional messages to get your attention. This, when done prayerfully and with the guidance and direction of the Holy Spirit CEO, is known as Inner Healing. Yes, the Lord really is *still* in the business of healing today!

(If there is a known trauma in your life that you are feeling in any way uncomfortable or anxious about, I would encourage you to seek out the help of a trusted Christian friend, a reputable Christian counselor, a

church that is competent in Sozo ministry, or a professional therapist or psychologist before attempting to revisit the trauma alone. If your Heart feels the Lord's Peace about going there, step gently and only do as much or as little as He tells you to do.)

chapter four

The Emotions

"I called to the Lord in my distress, and I cried to my God for help. From His temple He heard my voice, and my cry to Him reached His ears…" (Psalm 18:6, HCSB).

Journal Entry, 7th November, 2003: *"I've finally seen what my Emotions are like. They're all standing guard around my Heart, facing outwards; it's almost as if they pre-empt the messages from the Heart—I don't know if that's possible, but that's what I see.*

"My Heart is recovering, but it's still weak; and it's as if the Emotions have learned the Heart's signals and responses to the point where they see what's coming and, WHAM! They're out there, before the Heart has really processed what's going on.

"The experts say that a heightened emotional state is a sign of stress. I guess that fits! I feel like I'm cleaning up Darwin after cyclone Tracey—by myself, and the task is daunting… to say the least.

"So, my Emotions are like sentinels or guards. They have uniforms, and they are outside the door of the room where my Heart is recovering. I can't see if they are different colors, or shapes, or ranks—they're just there."

Who Are You, and What Do You Want?

The Emotions are quite possibly the least understood member of our boardroom. For some of us, the Emotions are an inconvenience; a necessary evil that we spend our time and energy trying to suppress. For others, the Emotions are a volatile force that cannot be ignored no matter how hard one might try. My own journey in understanding my Emotions has been informative, quite laborious at times, but also very rewarding.

You can see, reflected in the journal entry above, that dealing with the Emotions can be very overwhelming. Either they are so suppressed that they no longer have a voice at the boardroom table, or they are so out of control that no one else has a voice at the table. Neither way is helpful. So, what is the purpose of Emotions? Why did God create us with Emotions? Moreover, how do we control them?

As I mentioned in the previous chapter, Emotional issues essentially stem from the Heart. If everything that has ever happened to us is stored in the Heart, then it makes sense that *some* of what has happened to us will be stored in a place that we neither want, nor intend, to revisit often. Some things are buried so deep in our subconscious memory that we have no conscious recollection of them ever having happened. The problem is that when we find ourselves in a new situation that may stir some of the same Emotions in us, we react in quite surprising and, sometimes, disturbing ways. The only way that the Heart can alert us to the fact that it is hurting is to send a *message* in the form of a feeling, or Emotion. Let me give you an example…

Once Upon a Time…

My sixth-grade school camp was a weeklong adventure in a small town in country Victoria called Hall's Gap. The campsite was nestled at the foot of a mountain, and one of the activities that we all looked forward to was the day we got to hike to The Pinnacle—an elongated, rectangular shaped rock at the very top of the mountain. Now, as mountains go, this was not a huge one, but it took the better part of two hours to hike the trail and climb to the top of the rock; it only took an hour to come down again, because we mostly ran, hooting and hollering as only eleven and twelve-year-olds do. I had thoroughly enjoyed the afternoon's energetic activities with a group of my friends; laughing and joking with linked arms. I felt quite certain that these would be my friends for the rest of my whole entire *life*!

As we arrived back at the campsite, we passed two of the teachers, who were heading out to the local store. Earlier that day, my friend Tara and I had asked if we could ride along. We wanted another shot at finding a few gifts to take home with us. At that point, we both understood that the teachers had said *yes* to our request. So, when they said they were leaving right away, Tara and I hastened back to our cabin to collect our money. We then ran back, still laughing and joking to the parking lot to meet the teachers.

Well, as misunderstandings go, there had just been a monumental one. We were about to discover it in a rather awkward encounter at the car. You see, the teachers were only aware that I had wanted to go to the store; they had not understood that both of us had wanted to go. They'd invited a few other teachers to come along, thus leaving only one seat in the car for the short trip to the store.

Immediately feeling uncomfortable for my friend, I said it didn't matter, and I'd stay back. She insisted, however, that I go on without her. After the customary "Are you sure you don't mind?", she assured me that she didn't mind at all. Given that I really wanted to find some souvenirs, I was bundled into the car and off I went to the store.

When I came back to camp with my purchases in hand, trying very hard to chew and swallow a rather large chocolate candy that one of the teachers had kindly shared with me on the way home, I came to realize the precarious position I had placed myself in with my friends.

I exited the car, searching for my friends. I quickly found them standing at the edge of the parking lot, near the doors to the dining hall. I was oblivious to their hostile attitude right away—I didn't notice the folded arms, the disgusted and angry tilt to their heads or the snickers and snide remarks until I was almost right on top of them, still trying to clean the last of the chocolate from my teeth.

"Teacher's pet!" My friend Tara spat the words at me with all the venom she could muster.

"But—you told me to go!" I stammered in defense. I was genuinely confused and quite hurt by their response. There were about five of them in the group and, in one rehearsed motion, they all five tossed their hair and turned on their heels; they walked away and left me standing, awkwardly, with my bag from the store dangling lifelessly from my limp wrist.

Fast-forward a few decades. I never gave that incident another thought. Why would I? My friend Tara and I made up again at some point, and I moved on. *Until* I found myself asking the Lord one day *why* I always seemed to feel hurt and upset when my friends planned to do things without me? I'm a grown woman; I'm beyond this kind of schoolyard pettiness, aren't I?

My own perceived maturity aside, I kept crashing into this wall of emotional reaction, and it took me a little while to figure out why. If one of my friends mentioned that she had caught up with another of my friends for coffee, I was usually okay with it. If they were to casually mention that it happened on a day or time when *I was not available,* however, it would set off an emotional whirlwind in me that left me feeling ashamed, guilty, rejected, and selfish. I could not make sense of any of these Emotions in light of the simple fact that my friends had coffee without me.

UNDERSTANDING THE EMOTIONS.

There are a couple of things that are critically important to remember if we are to understand our Emotions. The first, I believe, is something you might not have given much consideration to before. Our Emotions are, in fact, *amoral*—which is to say that Emotions, in and of themselves, do not carry a moral value. They are not right or wrong—they just are.

Paul, quoting from Psalms 4:4, gives this admonition to us in Ephesians 4:26, *"Be angry, and do not sin" (HCSB)*. The NIV version says, *"In your anger, do not sin."* The NLT says, *"And don't sin by letting your anger control you."* He is not telling us that *being* angry is a sin; he is telling us to be careful and mindful of how we act when we *are angry*. The Bible records in several places that Jesus was angry—at the money changers and those selling in the temple complex (found in John 2:13), and at the death of Lazarus (read John 11:38 and following), so *being* angry clearly is not a sin. What we *do* when are angry can get us into trouble, but *feeling* the Emotion itself is not a sin.

The second thing to keep in mind is the nature of a reaction. A reaction is something that is uncontrolled, or uncontrollable, and it is usually something we are *not* expecting. When the Heart sends an Emotional message that results in a reaction, it is just that—a message. What we do with that message determines how we move forward. Therefore—when we find ourselves in a situation that produces Emotions that resemble in *any* way those buried Emotions, which were filed with a traumatic memory, the Heart *automatically* sends the same Emotional message it tried to send the first time.

For example—in the moment where my friends all turned their backs on me at sixth-grade camp, I felt gutted, fearful, alone, and lonely. I felt confused and misunderstood. All these Emotions go with the message of "rejection" that my Heart was trying to send me in the moment. Of course, I had no idea how to interpret those Emotions at the time. In the same moment that my friends flipped their hair and spun on their heels, that avalanche of Emotions came crashing over me, resulting in the near loss of the chocolate candy that was turning rather acidic in my belly, and a barely controllable flood of tears.

Jump forward again to my adult friends having coffee without me. Those same feelings of rejection, that I did not know how to deal with when I was twelve, were still buried in my Heart. The response of my adult friends, while nothing like the earlier response of my schoolgirl friends, triggered the same feelings of rejection in my Heart. Therefore my Heart, in keeping with the job it was created to do, sent the same message it had probably been trying to send me ever since that incident at sixth-grade camp—and I kept ignoring it because I couldn't understand what my Heart was trying to tell me.

The problem was that because I hadn't dealt with the original message, I had very little idea of how to deal with any subsequent messages that my Heart might send. The Heart doesn't just send the original message, it also sends extra's—all the other layers of traumatic and upsetting incidents that were never dealt with over the years—giving two, three, or twenty Emotional messages, all for the price of one.

You see, it's not enough to just *choose not to feel* certain Emotions. In some circumstances, yes—it's possible—but it can't be applied as a blanket choice for all occasions. Remember, Emotions are amoral. You can't always control an Emotional reaction because you don't know when it's coming. An Emotional reaction is simply the Heart shooting you a message, and you can't be aware of every message the Heart wants to send at any given moment. The more you practice hearing your Heart, the quicker you'll get to an understanding of what's going on; but, in the moment, you must learn to deal with the message in front of you. You can't always just *choose* it away.

What Am I Feeling?

So, what do we do with the Emotion once the Heart sends it? To make sense of the Emotional messages being sent in the current situation, we must first be able to identify the Emotions, or *decipher and receive the message* that our Heart is trying to send us. We must ask ourselves the question, *"What am I feeling about this situation?"*

There is something that is worth restating here: The Heart just wants to be heard. If it sends a message and you ignore it, the Heart will send it repeatedly until the message is received and it feels heard. For this reason, you may often find that there may be more than one Emotion trying to present itself. I encourage you to write down any Emotion that you can name; ask the Lord for His help if you are struggling to identify how you are feeling. Once you have deciphered the message and acknowledged that this is indeed how you are feeling, you can then ask the Lord to direct you, bringing you back to the memory of the *first time you received this message*—or the first time you felt these Emotions.

Sometimes, the memory will come quickly. If it takes time, it may indicate that a conversation with your Heart is needed so that you may move forward.

This was my process regarding my sixth-grade example. Granted, I have given it all to you in reverse order, but the Lord led me to that memory after I asked Him the question, "When was the first time I felt this?" (Specifically, in my case, those feelings of rejection that I described earlier).

I could identify that I was feeling rejected, worthless, and unimportant. I realized those feelings stemmed from guilt and shame—but I could not, for the life of me, figure why *those* emotions. Why *this* message? The message didn't feel like it fit the circumstances. So, I asked the Lord; but even when He showed me the memory, I couldn't work it out.

That is, until I asked Him the next question.

What Was the Lie?

The next question to ask the Lord, at this point, is *what did I begin to believe that was not true?* In other words—what lie did I believe about that circumstance or situation? When we believe a lie about something, there is a part of our Heart that gets wounded. Believing a lie may be the only way we can cope with, or process, the situation in the moment. The hurt that results from the combination of the circumstance and the lie is usually enough to cause us to lock away the memory of it in the deepest, darkest recesses of our subconscious and, as I said before, we often never revisit.

For me, the lie I believed at sixth-grade camp was that I did something terribly and shamefully wrong to cause my friends to react and treat me the way they did. I should never have gone, despite my friend's assurances that it was okay that I did. Their actions toward me that day, and for the days following, caused me to vow that *I would never again* give my friends cause to be upset with me, thus leaving me out of the group.

The problem with believing a lie is that we eventually end up believing more lies. To never upset my friends, I had to act in a way that pleased them, always. Otherwise, I was guilty of doing something terribly and shamefully wrong that caused them to be upset with me. My need to be included fed into the lie that I needed to please my friends continuously which, in turn, fed into the lie that something must be wrong with me if they chose not to spend time with me.

As you can well imagine, I spent many years miserably trying *not* to upset people, and then beating myself up when it was clear that I *had* upset people. Of course, as an adult, my Mind was constantly trying to convince the rest of my boardroom that this was foolish and unnecessary but, every time I found myself in a similar circumstance, my Heart would frantically send messages (Emotions) that told me the opposite.

Emotions can *feel* true. Therefore, when I felt left out, my own subjective truth told me that I *must* have done something terribly and shamefully wrong to cause my friends to organize that outing and not include me… you can see the impossible corner I kept backing myself into.

What Is Your Truth, Lord?

Thankfully, I didn't stay there. Over the years, it has become very clear to me that the Lord gave us Emotions so that we would have a way of recognizing the areas of our Heart that He wants to be invited into. An out of control Emotion lets me know the exact location of the next miracle the Lord wants to perform in my life, *if* I am willing to invite Him into that space.

Once the lie has been exposed, and my Heart can understand that the thing it has held onto for so long is a lie, I am then able to ask the Lord for His truth about the situation. By this stage of my journey, I was becoming more proficient in hearing from the Lord and interacting with Him in this kind of conversation, so you may notice that the conversation flows a little more smoothly than in some of my previous entries. We were created for relationship with Him. He wants to speak with us more than we want to hear from Him. I know this because if, *"God so loved the world that He gave His only Son…"* then it makes perfect sense that this same God would now want to cultivate a relationship with us. Anyway—here is how that whole conversation went:

Journal Entry, 2006: H: "*Okay Lord, I feel shame and guilt and rejection whenever my friends plan to do something without me; or when they make decisions and plans without including me. Why do I feel shame and guilt? Rejection I understand, but why the others? When was the first time I felt these things?*" *(He immediately brought to mind the memory described above.)*

"YOU FEEL THAT IT WAS YOUR FAULT—THAT YOU **MADE** YOUR FRIENDS ANGRY WITH YOU."

H: "But I did, didn't I? If I hadn't gone with the teachers, my friends would not have had cause to be angry."

"THEY FELT ANGRY BECAUSE THEY FELT LEFT OUT, NOT BECAUSE YOU WENT."

H: "Isn't that the same thing?"

"NO, IT'S NOT. THEIR HEARTS WERE SENDING MESSAGES OF THEIR OWN IN REACTION TO THE CIRCUMSTANCES THEY FOUND THEMSELVES IN."

H: "So it **wasn't** my fault that they were angry with me...?"

"NO, DEARHEART, IT WAS NOT YOUR FAULT!"

H: "I still don't understand why shame and guilt are so strongly felt, though. If it wasn't my fault, why did I feel so ashamed? I can still taste the chocolate goo in my mouth that wouldn't be swallowed; I couldn't speak or defend myself at all. I wore the blame for their anger and all I could do was cry."

"THAT WOULD BE ANOTHER LIE."

H: "Which—that **I wore the blame for their anger?**"

"YES. IF BLAME WERE TO BE ASSIGNED ANYWHERE, IT WAS WITH THE TEACHERS FOR PUTTING YOU IN THE POSITION IN THE FIRST PLACE. YOU ACCEPTED THE BLAME, BUT IT WAS NOT YOURS TO CARRY."

H: "So shame and guilt are so strong because of blame? They blamed me because I got to go and Tara didn't."

"YES."

H: "So if the blame wasn't mine to carry, then guilt and shame are miscommunications."

"GUILT AND SHAME ARE THE ONLY MESSAGES YOUR HEART KNOWS TO SEND. GUILT AND SHAME WERE SENT AS A REACTION TO THE LIE YOU BELIEVED."

H: "So what's the truth? If the lie is indeed a lie, and it wasn't my fault and I wasn't to blame, then what's the truth?"

"THE TRUTH IS, DEARHEART, THAT YOUR FRIENDS WERE IMMATURE. THEY REACTED OUT OF THEIR OWN HURT AND ASSIGNED BLAME WHERE IT DID NOT BELONG. THEY DID NOT SEE TRUTH, OR KNOW TRUTH, AND SO THEY COULD ONLY COMMUNICATE A LIE."

H: "I think I get it…"

"BUT?"

H: "Why do I still believe that I should have done something different? If I had seen the bigger picture; if I had chosen a different course of action, then I would have spared my friends feelings."

"YOU WERE ELEVEN YEARS OLD, DEARHEART! YOU DIDN'T KNOW ANY DIFFERENT YOURSELF."

H: "Perhaps not, but I'm not eleven any more. Now I do know better."

"BUT NOT IN THE CONTEXT OF TRUTH, AND NOT IN THE CONTEXT OF THAT MOMENT. YOU KNOW BETTER THAN TO HURT YOUR FRIENDS OUT OF YOUR OWN HURT, BUT YOU STILL HAVE NOT LEARNED THAT YOU ARE NOT ALWAYS RESPONSIBLE FOR THEIR HURTS."

H: "Even if I am involved in the situation or circumstance that hurt them?"

"THERE IS A DIFFERENCE BETWEEN BEING INVOLVED AND BEING RESPONSIBLE. WHEN YOU KNOW YOU HAVE BEEN **RESPONSIBLE** FOR SOMEONE'S HURT, HOW DO YOU FEEL?"

H: "Guilty and ashamed! I'm not seeing the difference?"

"WHAT DO YOU DO ABOUT IT?"

H: "I go and try and sort it out. Apologize. Make amends. Try and fix what I broke, if can."

"YOU FEEL MY CONVICTION WHEN YOU HAVE BEEN **RESPONSIBLE** FOR SOMEONE'S HURT. WHAT DOES MY CONVICTION FEEL LIKE?"

H: "Light, easy; specific. I know what I have to do, and how to do it."

"DO YOU STILL FEEL UNCOMFORTABLE? GUILTY? ASHAMED?"

H: "If I know it was my fault, yes, I still feel all of those things."

"BUT THOSE THINGS DON'T STOP YOU FROM ACTING TO RECONCILE WITH A PERSON?"

H: "No...they don't."

"WHAT DOES CONDEMNATION FEEL LIKE?"

H: "It feels heavy, paralyzing, generally confusing and really hard to figure out."

"CONDEMNATION SEEKS TO USE GUILT AND SHAME TO ITS ADVANTAGE. IT MAGNIFIES THE FEELINGS UNTIL THEY ARE ALL-CONSUMING. YOU KNOW PERFECTLY WELL HOW TO RESPOND TO THE MESSAGES OF GUILT AND SHAME IN THE LIGHT OF MY **CONVICTION**, BUT YOU SURRENDER TO THE PARALYZING NATURE OF GUILT AND SHAME UNDER THE SHADOW OF THE ENEMY'S CONDEMNATION. WHAT DOES MY WORD SAY ABOUT **CONDEMNATION**?"

H: "That "There is **no** condemnation for them in Christ Jesus..." (Romans 8:1). So, I have been listening to condemnation, as well as the lie?"

"IT WOULD SEEM THAT WAY. WHEN YOUR HEART SENDS A GUILT AND SHAME MESSAGE, WHAT SHOULD YOUR FIRST QUESTION BE?"

H: "I guess it would have to be- Does this guilt and shame carry with it conviction, or condemnation?"

"YES! EXACTLY RIGHT—AND IF IT CARRIES CONDEMNATION...?"

H: "Then I would have to ask why, and where it was coming from. So, the guilt and shame over causing my friends to be angry with me carries with it a large measure of condemnation, because I believed that it was entirely my fault and I accepted and carried blame that was not mine to carry."

"SO, WHAT IS THE TRUTH OF THAT SITUATION?"

H: "That I was caught in the middle of what wound up being an impossible position. Yes, my friends were hurt, but I was not responsible. I played a part, yes, and I guess I was able to apologize adequately for that, *because I made up with Tara eventually…"*

Do you see how that works? Any Emotion that the Heart sends out is either in *response* or in *reaction to* something. In this way, the Heart needs to learn to team up with the Conscience to send the Emotional message that partners with the conviction of the Holy Spirit, eliciting a Godly *response*. The alternative is that the Heart sends an Emotional message that is in *reaction* to condemnation and lies over which we seem to have little control.

Once we have learned to understand the messages that our Heart sends us and can deal with those Emotions in a Godly way, we see how He brings His healing touch to the wounded areas of our lives. We may travel a few times around the mountain before we can enjoy complete healing in some areas, but once the old wound has been cleaned out and healed, we find we can *choose to respond* from that place of healing, instead of *reacting* from a place of woundedness.

CONFESSION IS GOOD FOR THE SOUL…

Journal Entry, 4th May, 2004: "…*Lord, my attitude lately has been really bad; it's born out of the assumption that the feelings I have are founded on truth, and not on a lie. When I feel rejected; when I feel fear of being rejected; when I feel worthless and insignificant—when I allow these emotions to take up residence in my heart, and when I incorporate them into the way I live, I am not seeking You…*

"I don't see them for what they are. I don't see **anything** *in the light of Truth—I am letting the lies of the enemy dictate how I should live; but if You are the Lord of my life, then it is Your Truth that should determine the way I should live. So, Jesus, these are the things I feel—from my heart to Yours.*

"I feel insignificant and of no value. I feel rejected and not loved. I feel

*anger that is driven by fear, but it's a **powerless** anger. I get angry and frustrated when I believe I can do nothing to change my circumstances, that I must sit back and watch things unfold and then deal with the mess later.*

*"Lord, when anger comes from You, when it's a righteous anger, it is **powerful** because I can pray. I think I'm beginning to understand why You tell me to pray for people when I am angry at them. Praying when I am angry seems paradoxical, but if the anger that comes from fear is power**less**, then the soft, quiet anger that comes from You is power**ful**. When I pray for the person or situation from that place of quiet anger, it takes all the bluster out of the emotion and opens the way for You to work.*

"If I try to hang on to my Emotions for any reason, I give the enemy a foothold to come in and distort those Emotions, planting lies and resentment in my heart…"

Growing up, I picked up the idea somewhere that confession was not important to my spiritual health and wellbeing. I believe I thought for a long time, that "confession" meant that I had to tell God about what I did wrong (my sin). I should ask Him to forgive me for everything I did wrong, and then ask Him into my Heart. The process of confession and asking forgiveness was known as "salvation." If this was something I had to do on a regular basis that would be like asking Jesus into my Heart every day, which was silly, because I did that already.

Perhaps it was an immature understanding that I picked up and carried with me into adulthood. Maybe I heard someone say it once and understood it out of context. Whatever the causality of this understanding, I have come to the realization that it was wrong, at least in part.

Confession *is* telling God about what I did wrong and asking His forgiveness, but the implications of doing it or not doing it regularly are *huge*. Most of my conversations with the Lord include confession. My confession is prompted by His propensity for asking the right questions in the right order. I find myself coming into alignment with His way of thinking about things as I process my junk.

Speaking from experience, going for too long without confessing makes for a strained relationship with the Lord. Worse than that, the longer I go without it, the more prideful I tend to become, falsely assuring myself that my way of thinking is the right way. I become increasingly convinced that I'm right and don't *need* to confess anything—dangerous territory to be sure.

James 4:6 says, *"God resists the proud, but gives grace to the humble"(HCSB)*. If I am filled with pride…well, that's a disturbing thought. Confession is what *keeps* us humble. In any other relationship, if we are unable to show humility and ask someone for forgiveness, that relationship will suffer for the sake of our pride.

Confession says: "Wow, Lord, I've been doing this all wrong! I'm so sorry. Your way is so much better. Please forgive me…!" Confession is closely tied to *repentance*—changing my mind about what I believed was right and agreeing with what God says is right. I can't have one without the other. If I confess without repentance, I am only half way there, and repentance without confession is equally useless because what am I repenting of if I have not yet confessed?

In the discussion about our Emotions, confession is particularly pertinent because of one important truth: when I am able to hear my Heart and identify the Emotional message it has sent me, my Heart now *feels* heard. This means that it no longer must send that message. If you have small children, you will understand this concept. When Billy comes to you whining, complaining, or crying about the wrong that was done to him, he will often, in his emotional state, say things that would be inappropriate for you to act upon. "Johnny hit me with a stick! I think Johnny needs to be hit with a stick so he knows how it feels!" You have a choice of two responses. You can ignore Billy, in which case he will start whining louder and louder until he gains your attention, or you can sit and listen to him.

Now, you will not feel compelled to go out and hit young Johnny with a stick; but you will sit and talk to Billy about what happened. You will hear his grievances, gather information, and build a picture of what really happened. You will ask questions. Perhaps Billy will reveal that he *told* Johnny to try and hit him with the stick (true story). Perhaps Johnny was just being a bully but, either way, Billy wants and needs to be heard. Once he has been heard, his emotions settle down and he no longer feels the need to "Show Johnny how it feels."

In the same way, when I confess my Emotions and their effects on my life to the Lord, it takes a lot of the bluster out of the Emotion because in confessing how I am feeling and how I got to that place, I am ensuring that my Heart has been heard. Once my Heart has been heard, it does not need to intensify, or ramp up, or increase the volume of the message it is sending.

Without confession, it is far too easy for my Emotions to rule me. They become too big; I find myself focusing on how I feel about things and, therefore, I look for ways to alleviate (or perpetuate) how I feel. I make decisions based on Emotional outcomes, and I become quite volatile in my reactions to people and situations. The opposite can also be true. If I ignore my Emotions and treat them as inconvenient, insignificant, and of no value, I disregard any message my Heart tries to send me because those messages do not make sense.

If I receive an electrical bill in the mail, and I do not like the size of the number typed in the box that tells me how much I owe the electrical company, I *can* set it to one side and ignore it. I *can also*, if I wanted to, tear it up, put it in the trash, and pretend that I never received it. I *can*…but I won't. Why? Because if I do that, I know that the electrical company will just send me another bill. And another and another until I respond appropriately and pay the bill. I know that if I ignore that bill long enough, the electrical company will cut the power to my house and I will be without electricity, which is *way* more inconvenient than paying that exorbitant fee in the first place. If I still refuse to pay the electrical company, even after they cut off my lights, I know that they will hand the case over to the debt collectors and life will be made uncommonly difficult for me. So, I write a check and pay the bill and move on, perhaps now with a little more awareness of my electrical usage.

Ignoring my Emotions can have a similar impact. The Heart sends a message. I receive it, decide I don't really want to "pay that price"—I don't wish to feel that Emotion because it's inconvenient, illogical, and unpleasant—so I ignore it, minimize it, or bury it. Therefore, the Heart sends another message. This one is worded a little more strongly. I bury it. Heart sends another message…until I find myself super stressed out and bursting into tears at the drop of a hat, or blowing up in anger at the slightest provocation and apologizing all over myself after the fact, as if, "I'm so sorry, I don't know what got into me!" is going to erase the damage I caused.

There Is a Better Way…

Or, I could find a time and place to get quiet enough to take a good long look at the message the Heart sent. Perhaps not in the moment—Susanne Fengler used to always say, "Don't work on the roof while it's raining!" Wait until the sun comes out. Wait until the heat of the moment has died down. Then go through the process of identifying the Emotion and hearing what the Heart is saying.

The questions listed at the front of this chapter are a perfect starting point for getting to the root of the Heart's issues. The whole point of our Emotions is to show us what is in our Heart. They are a gift from the Lord because they point to the things He wants to heal, restore, or grow in us, leading us toward healing and wholeness.

The good news is that my Emotions are *mine*. Your Emotions are *yours*. No one can *make* me feel anything. The Emotion is a message letting me know what is going on in *my* Heart. I don't have to wait for the other person to stop doing what they were doing to stop feeling; I have complete control over my own Emotional well-being. I can lock myself away in a cupboard and not interact with any one for years at a time and I will *still* have Emotions. Believing that someone else is responsible for how I am feeling is simply not true.

Once we understand what the Emotions were created for and learn to work with them instead of burying them or letting them control us, we will find that our Emotions can be brought under the authority of the Holy Spirit CEO. Emotions can then become a helpful and respectful contributing member at the boardroom table.

Now It's Your Turn:

Every person on the planet has Emotions. The trick is being aware of them and learning to identify them. Some of us are *very* well acquainted with our Emotions; others of us may be a bit bewildered by the thought of having to name them. For those of you in that category, this may prove to be a bit of a challenge, but will also be quite helpful.

Think of a time when you felt a strong Emotion; it might be anger, or fear, or anxiety. Think about the circumstances that evoked that Emotion, and ask the Lord the questions already outlined in this chapter. If you are unable to identify the Emotion you are feeling, your first question for the Lord will simply be, **"Lord, what Emotion am I feeling right now?"** Allow some time and space for Him to answer. Use these questions as a springboard for getting a conversation started with the Lord. The format might look something like this:

*"Lord, I felt intense anxiety in that meeting yesterday afternoon. I want to learn how to listen to my Heart by deciphering my Emotions correctly. So please would You show me…***when was the first time I ever felt** *intense anxiety like that?"*

Record what the Lord shows you; it might be a memory; something you haven't thought about in years. He may also show you a composite of many memories. Go with the memory that surfaces, even if it seems irrelevant. Once you have your memory, you can move onto another question:

"Lord, where are You in this memory?" (This is particularly important, especially if the memory is a 'pre-conversion' memory—one from before you were saved. God is omnipresent, which means He is *everywhere, all the time*, and it is very helpful to know that He was present even when we were not aware of it.) Once He has revealed Himself to you, move onto the next question.

"Lord, what lie did I believe about myself, about You, or about others?" Identifying the lie will help you see why the Heart sent the message it sent. This is the point of injury for the Heart that needs God's healing touch. Once you have identified the lie, and your Heart understands and believes it to be a lie, you can ask:

"Lord, what is Your truth?" Our Heart will hold onto and treasure a lie until it believes there is something better to hold onto. I have found that it often helps if I ask the Lord for an exchange. I ask Him to show me a physical representation of the lie, and a physical representation of His truth, and then have my Heart "let go" of the lie so that I may grab hold of His truth.

Having worked through this exercise, you will find that the next time you find yourself in a situation that normally would have triggered intense anxiety, (or whatever your present Emotion may be) you can control the Emotion to a degree you never could have done before. As you reinforce the truth that the Lord imparted to you, you will find that you can control the Emotion to greater and greater degrees, until one day you will surprise yourself by responding without *any* of the previous Emotion. That's what inner healing is—allowing the Lord to speak into and heal those areas of Emotional hurt so that they no longer rule you or bully you into reacting out of woundedness.

chapter five

The Conscience

"This is how we are sure that we have come to know Him: by keeping His commands. The one who says, "I have come to know Him," yet doesn't keep His commands, is a liar, and the truth is not in him. But whoever keeps His word, truly in him the love of God is perfected. This is how we know we are in Him: The one who says he remains in Him should walk as He walked."
(1 John 2:3-6, HCSB)

Journal Entry, 2004: *"When I asked the Lord to show me my Conscience, the picture I saw was a likeness of my Dad, dressed up like Henry VIII. I was quite perturbed by that revelation, because I saw my Dad as neither religious nor as a tyrant.*

"He was, however, quite authoritative. I **hated** *whenever I did anything that displeased him, governing my behavior in a manner that would never disappoint him. If I knew something would not please him, I just wouldn't do it.*

"My Dad and my Granny were two very powerful motivators toward behaving myself in my growing up years. If I could not justify my actions to either one of them, then that action was just not worth the risk of taking.

"The overall impression I have of my Conscience is that it is "on guard" all the time, and very quick to beat me up or punish me for the smallest thing–authoritarian, one might say! The Conscience, while very

necessary to the building of our character, can be slippery to pin down."

The unregenerate Conscience can be a bully in the boardroom. Usually not out of any sense of malice or sinister intent, but mostly, out of the fear of doing something wrong. In the same way that a parent scolds a child for running out into a busy street, our Conscience scolds us for anything that falls outside of its scope of morality—it is usually born from fear for our well-being.

My Conscience has learned to lay low and fly under the radar, so to speak. My Conscience is a sneaky bully who beats me up over the smallest things…unless I recognize it and deal with it early. Learning the difference between conviction and condemnation is imperative in dealing with sneaky bullies. At great risk of laboring the point—the conviction of the Holy Spirit is light, liberating, and specific, always seeking to draw us closer to the heart of the Father. The condemnation of the enemy is heavy, exhausting, and demanding, driving us away from relationship with God. Condemnation is so generalized that it is impossible to bring focus to anything. This imposter is the counterfeit of conviction. When the Conscience doesn't know any better, it will partner with the counterfeit.

The unregenerate Conscience takes on a lot of responsibility that it really does not need to take on, becoming overactive and somewhat tyrannical in its approach to life. One of the things I have noticed about my Conscience is that it often takes it upon itself to turn an *external requirement* into an *internal obsession.*

For example, there is a difference between the external requirement that I be organized so that things run as smoothly as possible, and the internal obsession with "being organized" that may rule me or paralyze me, or in any other way restrict my day-to-day activities.

The external requirement that I be organized brings pressure to bear when I am not organized because things aren't done that need to be done. If I wake up and I have no clean clothes because I have not done any laundry this week, the pressure of needing clean clothes will motivate me toward getting the laundry done as soon as possible. External requirements may cause a low level of stress—namely "what am I going wear to work today!" Mostly, though, I am just going to get on with doing what must be done, chalking it up to experience...next time I'll get the laundry done earlier in the week.

Contrast this with an overactive Conscience peddling an internal obsession. If having the laundry done is not just a requirement but now also an obsession, then when the clothes pile up in the hamper my Conscience kicks into gear, goading my Heart and stirring up my Emotions. The stress of having no clean clothes to wear is now secondary to the dilemma of not living up to my own expectations. The obsession condemns and the Conscience bullies and I enter the day berating myself for not being better organized. The self-judgment that comes from this can be paralyzing and crippling.

Alternatively, the unregenerate Conscience can be so burned or seared that it no longer has a voice at the boardroom table. Paul warns Timothy in 1 Timothy 1:19 to keep his Conscience clear, saying that some have *"deliberately violated their conscience; as a result, their faith has been shipwrecked"* (NLT, emphasis mine). A little further on in this passage of scripture he cautions against teaching from, *"the hypocrisy of liars whose **consciences have been seared**"* (1 Timothy 4:2 HCSB, emphasis mine).

The question must then be asked, "How does one's Conscience become violated or seared? And how do we protect against it becoming so?" To answer that question, we must first understand some things about the Conscience.

Jiminy Crickets!

Our Conscience is not always an easily distinguishable voice. Unlike Pinocchio, we do not have the luxury of Jiminy Cricket sitting on our shoulder, urging us ever onward toward the better choice. For most of us, listening to our Conscience has become an exercise in mental gymnastics, especially in this era of ethical, moral, and political correctness.

On its own merit, our Conscience may be a reasonable guide, but it is not infallible. Unfortunately, if we have taught our Conscience the wrong things, it will hold us accountable to the wrong things—sometimes with less than desirable effects.

Our Conscience is shaped by the culture, society, family, and religion within which we are raised. In some Asian countries, it is considered inappropriate for a woman to touch a man's hand; in most western cultures, it is considered rude to refuse a handshake, whether the recipient is male or female. Which way is right? Depending on where and how you were brought up, this can become a *matter of conscience*. An Asian man's conscience may allow him to shake hands with a western woman but not with an Asian woman.

Let me throw another example your way. After my husband, Mark, and I had been dating for a few months, he invited me to come stay with him at his parent's house. My husband is the youngest of seven children, and was brought up in a family and a social culture quite different than the one in which I was raised. Meeting "the parents" for the first time was a big deal—doubly so because the occasion I had been invited to was the next youngest brother's wedding, and so there would be opportunity to meet the entire family. I was eager to make a good impression.

I have always enjoyed being creative, and usually have a project of some description on the go. So, when I threw in the scarf I was knitting to work on when we had a spare moment or two, I didn't think too hard about it. Being the youngest of seven kids meant that most of Mark's siblings were married with children of their own by the time I came on the scene. On the Sunday, following Saturday's wedding festivities, I found myself quite overwhelmed by the sheer volume of people that descended on Ma and Pa Appleyard's tiny seven roomed house (and that *includes* the bathroom, laundry, and kitchen!) I thought I'd be okay—I'm the oldest of five children, so having young kids around wasn't anything new for me. I was quite unprepared, however, for about a dozen of them, ranging in age between two and twelve years in addition to nineteen adults. To me, this felt more like a church picnic than a family gathering! When I felt I could steal away to a quiet corner of the lounge room (about three steps beyond the kitchen), and pick up my knitting for a few moments of reprieve, I jumped at the opportunity.

Only a few minutes into my solitude, Mark came looking for me. I was curled up in the chair near the fireplace, absorbed in my knitting. I didn't notice the look of confusion and concern across his face as he entered the room and saw me thus engaged.

"What are you doing?" He asked in a whisper.

I smiled up at him and replied, "Knitting! Thought I'd get some more of my scarf done." He came and sat next to me, nervously looking over his shoulder. I quickly picked up on his agitation.

"What's wrong?" I asked, now also whispering. I wondered what had gotten him so worried.

"You better put that away before Mum sees you," he said, picking up the ball of wool that had fallen at my feet. I was taken aback.

"Why?" I asked. I couldn't hide my confusion.

"Because!" *Oh, of course. That explains everything*, I thought.

"Because why?" I asked as he took the knitting needles from my hands and placed them, along with my yet unfinished scarf into the bag on the floor.

"It's Sunday!" Still whispering, he seemed a little annoyed with me that I hadn't put two and two together.

"Umm…okay." No—wait—*not* okay! "What's that got to do with anything?" He looked at me in utter confusion.

"You're not supposed to knit on Sundays!"

"*Why?*"

"I…I'm not sure why, but Mum always got mad at my sisters for knitting on Sundays. Just one of those things, I guess." He took me by the hand and led me back into the throng of family gathered around the table in the back room. I tried not to look too guilty for having just been caught knitting on Sunday.

I clearly managed to pull it off, because I was invited back again a few weekends later, and to this day I'm sure Ma never knew. On the Saturday night, the family gathered again for a barbeque dinner. (For those of you *not* familiar with this Aussie tradition, picture grilling out, not pulled pork). After dinner, someone pulled out a deck of cards and began a game of—something involving matchsticks and small change—not sure what exactly. Mark looked eager to join in the game and pulled me into the seat next to him. I leaned over and whispered,

"I'm not allowed to knit on Sundays, but you can play *cards*?" He grinned at me as he picked up the hand he had been dealt.

"Yeah…so?"

We discussed this at length, after the fact. In his family, it was a sin to knit on Sundays. No one knew exactly why; it just wasn't done.

In my family, it was a sin to play cards, especially for money. "Go Fish" or "Snap" were okay—but they weren't really considered hard core "card games." My Granny was the godliest woman I knew. She frowned on card games of any sort on Sundays, even Go Fish, but she would *always* knit on Sundays. I had even seen her knit *in church*, particularly if there was a conference going on. She said it helped her listen better.

What we had here was a simple disagreement of *Conscience*. Mark's Conscience bothered him that I was knitting on Sunday because he had been taught that it was wrong. My Conscience bothered me that he was playing card games for money, because I had been taught that *that* was wrong. Which one of us was right?

The Difference Between Us and Them

Another thing that is true of our Conscience is that it is unique to all human beings. No matter how primitive the civilization might be, the people within it have a common understanding or sense of right and wrong. Each people group, whether it be a city, a nation, or a tribe in the back woods of Papua New Guinea, have a set of rules that govern right and wrong behavior. The Conscience measures right and wrong against this set of rules…most of the time.

Pets, on the other hand, *do not* have a Conscience. They have instincts and are trained to *do* right or wrong as determined by the human that trains them, but they have no innate sense of what is right and what is wrong within themselves. The intended purpose of the pet determines the nature and predilection of spirit of the chosen animal.

For example, a mean spirited and aggressive German Shepherd is better suited as an attack dog than a child's companion in most instances. The police force would not choose a sweet-tempered lapdog to be trained as an attack dog for narcotics recovery.

Consider this, also—when your dog does something it is not allowed to do, such as taking the steak from the kitchen counter that you had set aside for dinner, or dig up your flowers in order to bury the bone from the steak it stole, that dog makes no attempt to hide the fact that it did those things. My dog will just wag her tail and give me that endearing doggy grin, as if to say, "I buried a bone—wanna' see?" She does not cower and hide until she hears my angry response to her escapades; it is not a matter of Conscience for her at that moment but a matter of survival, based on instinct.

People, on the other hand, are very good at hiding when they know they have done something wrong. Which of you reading these pages have ever had to sit down with a two-year-old child and teach him or her how to lie to duck punishment? *People* need no coaching to hide their wrongdoing.

Take the Log out of Your Own Eye First

In Romans 2:1-3, Paul speaks of our propensity to judge and the consequences of it. *"Therefore, any one of you who judges is without excuse. For when you judge another, you condemn yourself, since you, the judge, do the same things. We know that **God's** judgment on those who do such things is **based on truth**. Do you really think—anyone who judges those who do such things but do the same—that **you** will escape God's judgment?" (HCSB, emphasis mine).*

Further, in Romans 14:13-18, *"...Let us no longer criticize [or judge] one another. Instead decide never to put a stumbling block or pitfall in your brother's way. (I know and am personally persuaded by the Lord Jesus that nothing is unclean in itself. Still, to someone who considers it unclean, it is unclean). For if your brother is hurt by what you eat, you are no longer walking according to love [if you eat it in his presence or with his knowledge.]* **Do not destroy that one Christ died for** *by what you eat! Therefore, do not let your good be slandered, for the kingdom of God is not eating and drinking, but righteousness, peace, and joy in the Holy Spirit. Whoever serves Christ in this way is acceptable to God and approved by man" (HCSB, emphasis and extra brackets mine).*

Paul could have made his point equally by saying, "Do not destroy the one Christ died for by what you watch on television," or "by what you do for entertainment", or "by what you say," or any number of other things. For the Kingdom of God is not what you do or don't do, or what you do or don't say, it is righteousness, peace, and joy.

Jesus told His disciples that the greatest commandment was to *love God and to love people*. *"This is how the world will know that you are my disciples!" (John 13:35, HCSB).* You see—for most of us, our Conscience has been trained to align with rules and regulations. Both Jesus and Paul, here, are telling us to align our Conscience with *love*.

When we align our Conscience with rules and regulations, we become blind to our own shortcomings and failures regarding those rules and regulations. We fall into the trap of finding fault with those around us, while justifying our own rule-breaking actions. We become experts on getting around the rules, and we place ourselves as judge and jury over those whom we consider worse rule-breakers than ourselves.

When we align our Conscience with love, however, the rules don't change, they just fade away into insignificance. If love is my highest goal, I will not do anything to jeopardize the love that exists between me and another person. The rules and regulations are there to protect love, but if I keep my Conscience aligned with love, I no longer need to be concerned about keeping the rules—because the rules take care of themselves while I love.

Bearing these things in mind, it can be said that humans have an inbuilt system of checks and balances called the Conscience, which can be fine-tuned or detuned, to align with either God's statutes and decrees or with the enemy's warped worldview. The problem is, we don't always tune our Consciences to the correct frequency. Consequently, we can find ourselves, as a race of people or as individuals, doing things that God never would sanction as *right*. We can do something *wrong* and not have our Conscience bother us about it.

Keeping a Clear Conscience

The Apostle Paul, in 1 Corinthians 4:4, says that he has nothing bothering his Conscience…even though before his conversion, he was persecuting and executing Christians. How can this be the case? As Saul, he was raised and trained to be a rabbi and a Pharisee. Gamaliel, one of the leading Pharisees of the day, trained him in these disciplines. Believing the scriptures as he had been taught, Paul's mandate was to rid the Jewish landscape of anyone who would seek to undermine those scriptures, and Christians undermined pretty much everything that Saul and his teachers and mentors stood for; it was a *matter of conscience* that urged Saul to pursue these heretics and silence them.

Enter Jesus, and the encounter Paul experienced with Him on the Road to Damascus. Saul encounters radical grace, forgiveness, and mercy in a measure he has never encountered before. He begins to learn a new set of rules and principles to live by. He now can align his Conscience to the Heart of the Father—to love. Knowing he is forgiven for the wrongs he now acknowledges he has committed in the past, he moves forward in his new identity. There is nothing on his Conscience because his Conscience was keeping him in alignment to that which he thought was right at the time, which is the job that the unregenerate Conscience believes it is designed to do.

Our unregenerate Conscience works in two ways, the first of which is *in retrospect*. As a young child, we are taught right and wrong by our superiors—parents, teachers, pastors etc.—but if they didn't know truth, then some of what they taught was incorrect. At the age of three, we are taught that it is *wrong* to snatch a toy away from another child and that it is *right* to share our things. Perhaps we were punished for the immature act; a slap on the wrist, or time out, or something equally as impacting. The next time we were in that situation and were faced with the choice to share or not to share, our Conscience kicked into gear.

"Remember last time? You got into trouble for not sharing that toy. Do you want another timeout? Better let her have a go..."

The second way our unregenerate Conscience works is *progressively*. Each time we listen to the voice of our Conscience, it gets stronger and we are more likely to listen to it again the next time around. If we ignore the Conscience, however, and choose to snatch the toy away and suffer the consequences, the voice of the Conscience becomes weaker the next time around. In this way, we can burn or sear our Conscience—by not paying attention when it speaks. After a while, the Conscience remains unheard as we continue to make choices that go against what we were taught is right.

"Trust in the Lord with all your heart, and do not rely on your own understanding; think about Him in all your ways, and He will guide you

on the right paths" (Proverbs 3:5-6, HCSB). I tend to think that we get ourselves into trouble over matters of Conscience because we far too often lean on our own understanding of things. If our Mind is a strong voice in our boardroom, then it will quickly and easily team up with the Conscience to give a logical, rational explanation for our actions or inaction. The voice of the Conscience gets louder (or softer, depending on how well we listen) on that specific issue until our character is shaped by the resulting belief and the behavior that stems from it.

For instance: A man who believes that his wife should be subservient to his desires and that she needs to be punished when she is not, will not be bothered by his Conscience if he beats her—no matter how *wrong* anyone else might think he is. His Conscience is seared and no longer has a voice. His character has been shaped by his belief. He no longer feels the need to listen to *any* voice that tells him otherwise.

The man who knows that it is wrong to beat his wife, but who has an issue with anger and claims he was provoked by her to do it, may have an attack of Conscience after the fact, trying hard to "make things up to her" in the following days. His character has been shaped by his conflicting beliefs, the first being that it is wrong to beat his wife, but the second belief states that she provoked him to the action. He swings between anger and remorse as his Conscience tries to make sense of the conflicting beliefs.

Trying to figure this out, aside from the Holy Spirit, will keep us on the same treadmill, going around the same mountain, revisiting the same issues over and over again—*until* we learn to submit to the Lordship of Jesus by leaning to *His* understanding. We must allow Him to be our measure of right and wrong, and align our Conscience to *His* way of doing things.

Think about Him in All your Ways

So how do we make sure that our Conscience is aligned correctly? Our Conscience tends to be *experience focused* rather than *God focused*, unless we actively seek to focus it on God. If our Conscience is focused on our past experiences as the measure of right and wrong, it often misses God's *Heart* for us in the lesson we learned. Left to its own devices, the Conscience will lean on its own understanding of the circumstances based on previous experiences.

Remember the incident at my sixth-grade camp? Along the way I realized that because of that experience, my Conscience was constantly reminding me that I *shouldn't* upset my friends in any way. The catch cry of the Conscience is *"Should! Shouldn't! Must! Mustn't! Ought! Ought not!"* Realign or reprogram the Conscience to measure right and wrong according to the heart of God—according to *love*—and we begin to see how God intended the Conscience to work in the first place—to reflect *His* nature and character.

A healthy, God-aligned Conscience will eventually work itself out of a job. Of course, we will always need it. Each new situation that we find ourselves in will require some level of Conscience involvement, but as the Conscience learns to team up with the Holy Spirit CEO to listen to and bring His conviction, it also learns to work with our Human Spirit to convert the lessons we learn along the way into good and godly *character*.

1 John 3:18-22 says, *"Little children, we must not love with word or speech, but with truth and action. This is how we will know we belong to the truth **and will convince our conscience in His presence, even if our conscience condemns us,** that **God is greater than our conscience** and He knows all things. Dear friends, if our conscience doesn't condemn us, we have confidence before God and can receive whatever we ask from Him **because we keep His commands and do what is pleasing in His sight"** (HCSB, emphasis mine).

God's children will not continue to sin once sin is revealed as sin. We do not live a lifestyle deliberately choosing to sin. We may sin in ignorance, not recognizing that what we are doing is sinful; we may even choose to sin because we are *deceived* into thinking or believing that what we are doing is the right thing; but God's children will *run* from sin once they know it to *be* sin. That is the work of an aligned Conscience. In partnership with the Holy Spirit CEO, who brings conviction, we can confidently trust that God will be *"faithful and righteous to forgive us our sins and to cleanse us from all unrighteousness"* if we confess our sins to Him. (See 1 John 1:9, HCSB).

Do you know that when Jesus walked this earth He was never bothered by His Conscience? That's because He got His measurement of right and wrong from God, not from the rabbi's, or His parents, or His friends. Yes—all these people would have had necessary input into His life, but the ultimate authority on right and wrong for Jesus was the Father. He only ever did and said what the Father showed Him and told Him. (See John 5:19; John 12:49). He is our example and our yardstick. If our Conscience is pricking us over a particular issue, our first port of call is to ask the Father, "Is this how *You* see this situation? If not, how *do* You see this situation?" Then trust what He tells you, even if it sounds different to what you always thought.

In the Beginning

Once upon a time, when the earth was still very young, God placed man and woman into the garden He had created. You are, no doubt, familiar with the story. Look at Genesis Chapter 2:15-17, *"The LORD God took the man and placed him in the Garden of Eden to work it and watch over it. And the LORD God commanded the man, 'You are free to eat from any tree of the garden, but you must not eat from the tree of the Knowledge of Good and Evil, for on the day that you eat from it, you will surely die.'"* (HCSB).

Whether you see this account in Genesis as metaphorical or literal, there are many very relevant things we can take from the account of the fall of man in the Garden of Eden. In these few verses, we can see that God gave the man a job to do. He was to look after, or tend, the garden. God also gave the man freedom—he was *free to eat* from any other tree, just not the Tree of the Knowledge of Good and Evil. Mankind was given the freedom to choose whether he would obey God's command, or not.

We all know that the man and the woman chose to disobey the command, eating from the forbidden tree. The fall happened and now all of creation suffers the consequences of their decision.

How many of us have had the thought, no matter how fleeting, that "*I wouldn't have eaten that fruit.*"? The truth is, we all would have. In fact, we all *do*. Every day. Every time we decide right and wrong for ourselves, without consulting the Lord for His opinion of what is right and wrong, *we eat from the Tree of the Knowledge of Good and Evil.* That was the fullness of Adam and Eve's sin. Not only did they disobey God's command, they also put themselves in the place of judgment between good and evil. Any time we put ourselves in that place, we are taking a place that belongs only to God, equating ourselves with God, or worse—exalting ourselves above God. When Lucifer did that, he was cast out of heaven—just sayin'.

Eve's desire was to be more like God, which is not a wrong thing, but she was deceived into thinking that her transformation into His likeness could be achieved through eating the fruit that God forbade them to eat. Transformation into His likeness down the pathway of *obedience* would have gained for her the goal she was seeking. What would have happened, do you think, if Adam had stepped in, taken Eve by the hand and gone to speak with God? Even *after* she had eaten the fruit, I believe that God just might have forgiven her, and they both would have learned a valuable lesson in obedience.

Remember, the Bible records that the point of the fall, the point of no return, was right after Adam ate of the fruit. Genesis 3:6, "*Then the woman saw that the tree was good for food and delightful to look at, and that it was desirable for obtaining wisdom. So, she took some of it and ate it; she also handed some to her husband,* **who was with her,** *and he ate it.* **Then the eyes of both of them were opened, and they knew** *that they were naked; so they sewed fig-leaves together and made loin cloths for themselves..." (HCSB, emphasis mine).*

Here's another thought: What would have happened if, instead of taking all that time to figure out how to sew fig-leaves together to cover their nakedness, they went straight to God and confessed what they had done? I understand; it's all semantics, but the point remains—Adam and Eve stepped into a role that belongs solely to God and, in so doing, they placed more value on their own judgment of right and wrong than they did on His. The good news is, that when we go to God in repentance and confess that we took His place of judgment in any given situation, He *will* forgive us. That is news worth celebrating!

Now It's Your Turn

Our Conscience, when submitted to the Holy Spirit CEO of our boardroom, is one of the most helpful tools we have. When we tune our Conscience into the correct frequency—going to God for our verdicts and conclusions on what is right and what is wrong—we learn the lessons we need to learn about the predicaments in which we find ourselves. We can do that, *because* we have the Holy Spirit CEO to whom we may turn. The first humans in the Garden of Eden had *God Himself* walking with them every day, and they still got it wrong! Don't be so hard on yourself when you fall. The more you practice going to God, the more you will default to it as you grow.

So, by now you know the drill. Find yourself a quiet place and time, and get ready for a conversation with your heavenly Father. Make a cup of coffee; get out your journal and turn off the phone. Take a moment to recognize His presence with you. Praise Him, adore Him, and practice quieting your Heart and Mind to *be still* in His presence. Ask the Lord, "How do *You* see my Conscience?" Ask Him where you need to be aware of stepping into judgment for yourself, and how would He have you change that tendency?

Record what He tells you and be prepared to ask questions about it, always with the goal of pursuing a dialogue with Him. Always submit your Conscience to the agenda of the Holy Spirit CEO, ensuring that it partners with conviction, not condemnation. The job of the Holy Spirit is to lead us into all truth; it is the job of the Conscience to follow Him.

---
chapter six

THE WILL

"Give me life in accordance with Your faithful love, and I will obey the decree You have spoken." (Psalm 119:88, HCSB)

Journal Entry, 23rd November, 2003: *"…My Will is a robot, not unlike that bunny in the ad on the television, whose batteries kept running out…"*

In Australia, years ago, there was an advertisement for batteries. The original ad showed two pink toy rabbits beating little drums. In this widely viewed commercial, the powerful new battery powered one rabbit, while the other rabbit was powered by a competitor's inferior brand. The scenario showed the new, improved brand of battery powering the bunny, as he continued happily beating his drum for hours and hours. The competing brand showed its bunny going slower and slower until he finally he ran out of power and stopped.

Over the years, the ad campaign gained traction and this favored brand began to show the staying power of its product through the increasingly heroic actions of that little pink bunny. His drum was discarded and replaced with an Olympic running uniform; real-time toy bunnies were upgraded to real-looking computer-generated bunnies that ran around the country, beating all the other computer-generated competition. I remember being quite entertained by the exploits of this high-energy bunny.

This first glimpse of my Will was not as entertaining. My not-so-high-energy bunny—my Will—was the one whose batteries kept running out. Mine was the competing brand bunny, who kept being left behind, who never finished the race, and who was always last because it kept running out of steam.

Discovering that my Will had no "get up and go!" was no new revelation. I think I've always struggled with motivation at some level. I remember my Mother telling me that I needed to learn "stickability"—her euphemism for *perseverance*. We seemed to have an ongoing conversation about it whenever *she* thought I should be practicing the piano, and *I* thought I wanted to do something else.

I enjoyed playing the piano—if I got to play what *I* wanted to play. I had a hard time disciplining myself to practice the things that my teacher wanted me to play. Mum's "stickability" speeches were predictable in their deliverance and permanent in my memory, so much so, that I now hear the same conversation being repeated in my own house, with my own daughter—some 30 years later—as I urge and encourage her to practice her violin.

The condition of our Will is largely influenced by the ways we were taught to submit to authority during our formative years. As with any other area of our development, the things we were taught by the people we respected in our lives were not always the truth; and we will likely perpetuate some of the same untruths in raising the next generation—unless we can learn to submit our Will to God and learn a better way.

Our Will can be damaged, hurt, or crippled by childhood trauma or those things that our Heart has *perceived* as being traumatic. The two most sensitive times of development are said to be when we are around two years of age and the teenage years. Proverbs 22:6 says, *"Teach a youth about the way he should go; even when he is old, he will not depart from it" (HCSB)*. While there are many far more educated than me who have expounded on this short verse, to me, the most obvious meaning is that if you train a child to do certain things when they are young, those things will stick, even to old age; whether they be for good or for evil.

Every child is different. We all have different personalities and tendencies. Any parent will tell you there is no "one size fits all" method of raising children. You have to get to know your child well in order to parent them well. So, if as a young child who was particularly outgoing and gregarious, you were raised by parents who believed that children should be seen and not heard, you would have learned some "truths" that affected your Will to some measure.

Conversely, if you were a shy child raised by outgoing parents, the same would be true. The Will can be broken and crushed; it can learn to be its own expert and develop a prideful tendency; it can be indecisive or it can know little restraint. All of this is dependent upon the environment in which you were raised. Even those of us who had "charmed" childhoods will still have faulty thought processes embedded somewhere that will affect our Will, because none of us were raised by perfect parents.

Our Will is also influenced by the condition of the other members of our boardroom. For most of us it is true that, along the way, the Will has carried out wrong decisions as dictated by the other strong voices in our boardroom. Confusion arises because we find ourselves stuck in self-destructive cycles, even while we know that these cycles are unhelpful and unhealthy.

When the Will follows the wrong leader in the boardroom, the result is procrastination, inertia, or remaining "stuck" in certain areas of our growth or spiritual development. There are always positive and negative gratifications going on in the boardroom. For example: Have you ever been dieting because you know you need to lose weight, but you *really* like food? Disciplining yourself to eat right will work great as long as the Will is following the Mind, which says, "You know you need to eat right so you can get your weight under control!"

That discipline goes down the drain when the voice of the Heart jumps in with its two cents worth, "But you *deserve* to treat yourself! You've had such a hard day!" When the Will is unable to identify its own unhealthy tendencies, we stay trapped in our own, equally unhealthy, self-gratification cycles.

Who Gets the Vote?

The *unregenerate* Will is that board member who will vote with the loudest or most persuasive voice at the boardroom table. In this way, it becomes a floating or swinging voter in any given circumstance and will execute whatever decision is made at the time.

The *broken* Will is the Will which has been exposed to such harsh authority—real or perceived—that it no longer believes it has any say in its own actions. The broken Will requires healing from the Lord in much the same way as the broken or hurting Heart and needs to be led gently and tenderly toward wholeness. The broken Will is unable to move beyond its own limitations; the unregenerate Will is immature in its actions and dealings with the other board members.

Because of this, while it is easy to see that we have no willpower in a particular situation, it is harder to see *why*, because in order to find out why we have no willpower to carry out a certain task, we first must understand *which board member our Will is voting with*.

If, getting back to the dieting example, we are having a war between our Heart and our Mind over what we eat, we can find ourselves behaving erratically, first carrying out what the Mind wants, and then doing an about face and obeying the orders of the Heart. Or we might find that our Will shuts down altogether, and we lack the motivation to do anything until the issue is resolved between the two.

The Will *does* have a voice of its own, however, but unless it is submitted to the Holy Spirit CEO, it tends to swing from one extreme to the other—either being too overwhelmed to act or so determined to act that it won't be dissuaded from its course. The unregenerate Will can be unwilling to do the tedious tasks of changing or taking risks—tedious because anything that doesn't come easily is considered not worth the effort; anything that does not give instant results is quickly thrown into the "too-hard" basket.

In this way, our Will can sabotage, sidetrack, or block our successes. These are signs of an unhealthy Will. If the Mind says, "That's got too many calories! We're not eating that!" The Will says, "Yeah! We're not eating that!" If the Heart then chimes in and says, "Yes—we *are*, because I'm hurting and I need this to make me feel better!", the Will says, "Yeah! We need to feel better!" If the Conscience says, "We *can't* do that because it will make us gain weight and I have to weigh-in tomorrow! We'll get into trouble!", the Will says, "Yeah! We'll get into trouble…but we need to feel better…even if it *is* fattening…! So, what is it I'm doing, again?"

Getting Motivated

I discovered some time back that *motivation is a byproduct of action.* Just sitting around and waiting for motivation to hit you before you get up and *do* something is like waiting for gold coins to drop out of the sky and into your lap; it's really not very likely to happen. Just thinking about losing weight isn't going to shed the pounds. The scales will make that painfully obvious.

If I believe that motivation comes first, then I'm going to wait a long time before anything gets done. Paradoxically, if I get up and begin the task that I am lacking motivation for, I am suddenly more motivated to finish it—especially if I start small.

I know I'm not going to lose ten pounds in the first few days. So, starting with being more aware of the size of each meal I eat is a good place to begin. Then I can move onto switching out the unhealthy for the healthy. As I make the changes and recognize the value of those changes, I am more motivated to stick to those changes. The decreasing number on the scale each week at weigh-in time reflects the changes, keeping me motivated.

Here's another example: My dislike for cleaning my room as a kid carried over into adulthood and became a dislike for cleaning my house. These days, I know that if I start small—start with unloading the dishwasher, for example, *then* move onto loading the dirty dishes back in, wiping down the countertops, the task doesn't seem as daunting. Over the years, I have learned that it only needs to take ten minutes. I now realize it won't take me two hours unless I listen to my Heart—which really isn't into the task in the first place. Then it might take me three hours to complete the simple task.

Once my Will learns that motivation is a *byproduct* of action, it can learn healthy ways of handling the frustration that comes when obstacles block progress. The healthy Will, as the executive secretary, also plays the role of project manager. Once the board member with the problem has been identified, the Will can execute the plans already put in place by the board for just such moments of crisis.

When the Heart, the Mind, or the Conscience has an issue, the Will ensures that said board member has the time and the space to sit and talk with the Holy Spirit CEO and sort out the issue. Once the issue has been dealt with, the Will is then able to get on with the task of carrying out the decisions of the boardroom, free of obstacles or hindrances.

The Will's job is to decide, "Will I or won't I sit down and spend time with the Lord on this matter today?" If the Will decides not to, then you have to ask the question, "Why not? What else are you going to do?" The answer to those questions will help lead you to the board member responsible for hijacking the Will.

In Colossians chapter three, verse nine and following, Paul gives this exhortation: *"Do not lie to one another, since you have **put off** the old self with its practices and have **put on** the new self. You are **being re-***

***newed** in knowledge according to the image of your Creator.... Therefore, God's chosen ones, holy and loved, **put on** heartfelt compassion, kindness, humility, gentleness, and patience... Above all, **put on** love—the perfect bond of unity... **And whatever you do, in word or in deed, do everything in the name of the Lord Jesus**, giving thanks to God the Father through Him"* (HCSB, emphasis mine).

Did you notice how many verbs or "doing words" are in that passage? Paul is not merely extending an invitation to passively wait for these things to overtake you. All those words mean that you have to make a deliberate choice in order to make it happen—a deliberate and intentional act of your Will.

If you awakened tomorrow morning to find that all your clothes had been laid out for you at the end of your bed—let's say you even stopped to admire them for a moment or two—but then did nothing about putting them on, everyone outside your house would notice that you forgot to get dressed. You might be able to explain to the lady on the bus that you had a snappy, three-piece suit, complete with matching tie and socks, all laid out neatly for you. This explanation would be offered, however, while you are sitting on the bus in your pajama pants.

No one cares what you're *not* wearing. They are more focused on what you *are* wearing. If you want people to notice the suit, *you have to do something about putting it on*. Take off your pajama pants, pick up the suit pants and step into them, one leg at a time. In the same fashion, you *put on* the shirt, one arm at a time, button it, *put on* the tie, and repeat the process with the jacket. Now people can see and appreciate the snappiness of your suit.

When it comes to *putting on* love, though, we somehow think that if we read about it this morning over breakfast, it will somehow cling to us without us having to *do* anything. So, why did Paul tell us to "put on" or "clothe yourself with" heartfelt compassion, humility, kindness, gentleness, and patience? Because he knew that, for most of us, it is a deliberate act of our Will to be kind, compassionate, and humble enough to forgive one another. We must make a choice—will I obey my hurting

Heart in this instance, or will I choose to obey the Holy Spirit CEO and forgive?

Sometimes it is the Will, itself, that needs to sit and talk with the Holy Spirit CEO. This can be a harder kind of inertia to overcome, as the broken Will—and sometimes the unregenerate Will—needs an outside force to get it moving forward.

As with any board of any company or business around the world, there must be some agreed upon protocols or pre-decided courses of action, for certain eventualities. The process is better executed if everyone knows that *this* is the prearranged course of action, leaving no time wasted on discussion or argument. When the Will is the recalcitrant member, and the one that is holding up the process of moving forward, there needs to be a similar, prearranged protocol.

As soon as it is determined that it is indeed the *Will* that has the problem, then everyone around the table knows what needs to be done. *No matter what else is on the agenda for this day, the Will needs time with the Lord*, and we're not just talking your regular 20 minutes of journal time. There is a glaring need for a cancel-all-calls, turn-off-your-cellphone, and-lie-on-the-floor-with-the-worship-music-playing-and-your-Bible-and-journal-close-to-hand type of journal time. No interruptions. You *have* to get this right, or you'll stay stuck for *years*, sometimes even decades. We don't have that kind of time to waste.

There are times in life where being stuck feels a bit like the chicken and the egg conundrum: Which comes first? If it is a choice of our Will to get the conversation going, but it is our Will that doesn't seem to *want* to get the conversation going, what is there for us to do?

Have you ever noticed, of yourself or others, that you can be totally uninterested in doing something one moment, and in the next instance you're ready and raring to go? For example, I may have no willpower whatsoever to go to a church function, but if in the next moment, a friend calls and asks if I'd like to go and visit that awesome new little chocolate shop that just opened downtown, I'm in! Interest and curiosity are often mistaken for motivation, and often when we think we lack motivation, we are in fact lacking interest.

The interest of our Will can be piqued, but that doesn't mean we are now motivated. Remember, motivation is a byproduct of action. We can become very active doing everything *but* the thing we need to be doing, thus hiding the fact that we lack motivation in that particular area. Until we engage the thing we lack motivation for, we will remain unmotivated to do it.

Enter the prearranged protocol. As soon as we realize that we are avoiding spending time with our Holy Spirit CEO, then we need to get tough with our Will and hold it accountable to the prearranged protocol. Our Bible time may begin slowly, painfully, and it might take time to ignite our interest in the process, but we do it because there is an agreement between our Will and the Holy Spirit CEO that this is how we will deal with inertia.

Now—What was That Thing I was Going to Do?

Let me give you a frank and honest example of how this actually works. As recently as the writing of this book, I have had to deal with my Will. Almost from the first weeks I started teaching this material over ten years ago, the Lord, my husband, group members, my co-leaders at church, my friends, and even random strangers with whom I have had the privilege of sharing this information on the boardroom, have all been urging me to write it down.

The problem was that I thought myself unworthy and unqualified to complete such a task. In this conversation with Holy Spirit CEO, I denoted the combined voices of the Heart, the Mind and possibly even the Conscience as "W," because these were the voices that the Will was listening to and acting upon.

Ongoing conversation with the Lord, November, 2015:
W: *"There are plenty of others way more qualified than I am to write about this."*
"BUT I AM ASKING YOU TO DO IT."
W: *"I know, but I can't write this book—I have too many other responsibilities!"*
"YOU CAN DO ALL THINGS THROUGH ME."
W: *"If I take time out to write, then something else will suffer. I won't be as available for my kids, my husband, or my friends."*
"TRUST ME…"
W: *"What if I say something stupid/wrong/heretical?"*
"TRUST ME TO TELL YOU WHAT TO WRITE."
W: *"What if I can't ever get it finished? What if no one wants to read it? I'm not well-known—who's even going to give it a glance?"*
"YOU WILL; THEY WILL; AND YOU COULD WELL BE AFTER THIS. YOU MIGHT BE SURPRISED."

I began to say, *Yes, Lord, I'll do it!*; but I couldn't say *No* to other things. I would block out days in my schedule to devote to writing and would end up doing housework, or ministry, or having lunch with a friend, or reading—because that pile of books I'm supposed to be reading is not getting any smaller.

"WHO SAYS YOU HAVE TO READ ALL THOSE, ANYWAY?"
W: *"Well, they'll be helpful in gaining perspective/for my spiritual growth/for personal awareness…so I know what I'm actually trying to write about…"*

If you're any kind of procrastinator, like me, you will be quite familiar with the excuses and the reasons and the endless explanations and rationalizations that one can come up with to avoid that which we know we must do. A quick poll around the boardroom table revealed that neither my Mind nor my Heart believed that I was capable or qualified to write a book. My Conscience was more concerned about the time it would take away from family. My Emotions, while a little raw from other unrelated recent events, were overreacting to the perceived pressure to get it done. My Body was tired and frequently shut down on me any quiet moment I managed to set aside—reading, writing, even doing bookwork and banking paperwork. I would find myself nodding off, so I went through the checklist. Am I eating right? Sleeping enough? Staying hydrated? Taking my vitamins? Check, check, check, and check…

The problem, I soon discovered, was that even once I had worked through the issues and had the board on my side, my *Will* was not surrendered to the Holy Spirit. When any of the board members remain unsurrendered, it usually boils down to an issue of *trust*.

Just over *ten years* have passed since I *know* the Lord was nudging me toward this task. Yes—I am aware that His timing is perfect, but sometimes He will put His perfect timing on hold while He waits for us to get with the program. As soon as we do, *voilà*—it's His perfect timing. I can beat myself up for wasting so much time, or I can get on with the job—evidenced by the fact that you are holding a completed work in your hands at this moment—and trust Him that my eventual obedience will have the impact He intended from the outset. There is no expiration date on surrender. He will accept it from you any moment you are willing to give it to Him.

I Surrender All

In today's vernacular, the word "surrender" brings with it the connotations and the understanding of defeat, forfeit, yielding to a stronger opponent, or losing a battle or game. Surrender is unthinkable when winning is everything, because it carries with it the idea of weakness, *and yet,* **surrender is the very thing that God asks of our Will.**

The truth is that everyone surrenders to something, and whatever we surrender to, that thing empowers us. If we surrender to anger, anger empowers us to be angry. If we surrender to hurt and hopelessness, then hurt and hopelessness empower us to be hurt and hopeless. I surrendered to procrastination, and procrastination empowered me to procrastinate. We are free to surrender to anything we choose, but once that choice is made, we are *not* free of the consequences of what we surrender to in this battle.

When we choose to act out of anger, hurt, pride, or anything else, we will be subject to the consequences of our actions and in many cases, so will others. The willful following of these things stop God's blessing on our lives, and He must sometimes challenge our pride, usually through painful revelation and circumstance, in order to change our Will.

Contrary to popular opinion, surrendering to God is not equal to fatalism—"it will all work out in the end, no matter what I do". Nor is it an excuse for laziness, passive resignation, or accepting the status quo—"I'm just waiting on the Lord…"; "God hasn't given me an answer yet, so I'm just in this holding pattern until He does."; "Well, nothing's changing, so I guess this must be His Will." Puh-lease!! Don't blame God for your own inability to get up and do something (spoken with authority from one who finally recognized she had to get up and do something).

Surrender makes us useable in His hands, giving us peace to accept His Will in everything because *our* Will has learned to trust His love. William Booth, the founder of the Salvation Army, was quoted as saying, "The greatness of a Man's power is in the measure of his surrender." There is *nothing* more powerful than a surrendered life in the hands of God. Surrender, however, is a lifetime goal; it will never be achieved in a single session or in the completion of a program.

Recognizing the symptoms of inertia—lack of motivation, lack of interest, busyness in some areas while isolating ourselves in other areas, and the realization that we are stuck in our spiritual growth and development—this is the big red flag. The big red flag lets us know it's time to suck it up, put on our grown up pants, and do the thing we don't feel like doing for the good of the whole boardroom.

Once the Will aligns itself with the Holy Spirit CEO, there is a sense of relief among the other members, because *now*—no matter how hard it is—there is a plan and we are moving forward. For all of us, there is a moment of decision to surrender, and then there is the daily, moment-by-moment *practice* of surrender—which is an attitude and a choice of our Will.

Now It's Your Turn

Typically speaking, any foray into the boardroom begins with an act of the Will. Whether it is an act of obedience or mere curiosity, is of little importance in the beginning. Sometimes the Will is just curious to find out, "What would happen if all of this were actually true and one could converse with one's inner self?" So, it would be safe to say, at the outset, that the Will is usually one hundred percent on board…in the beginning.

If, as I have said, any other board member is not willing to join in the conversation, the Will can, and will, change its vote and you might find yourself suddenly less inclined to continue. Remember, the Will is a floating voter and will support the strongest voice in the boardroom, regardless of logic or previous loyalties.

The choice to sit and spend time with the Lord is an act of your Will, so be encouraged by that small victory—the next steps will be easier because of this choice. You may find it necessary to work with one or more of the other board members in order to get to the reason the Will is unwilling if you have identified that as a problem.

I wrote earlier that when any of the board members remain unsurrendered it usually boils down to an issue of trust, or more accurately—a *lack* of trust between the board members and the Holy Spirit

CEO. We must learn to rebuild the trust in our boardroom if we are to move forward, and this means we must be willing to explore the reasons why we *don't* trust. You may find it helpful to poll the board members, asking each one in turn, "Do you trust the Holy Spirit CEO?" If the answer is *no*, then press harder. Ask yourself the hard questions. Don't be afraid to answer honestly, and don't try to sugarcoat or spiritualize your answers. John 8:32 says, *"You will know the truth, and the truth will set you free"* (HCSB). Allow your board members to speak honestly, and invite the Holy Spirit CEO into the conversation.

Begin, as usual, by praising Him for the gift of your Will. If you already know of a weakness in this area, confess this to the Lord and ask His forgiveness. Then ask the question, *"Lord, how do You see my Will?"* Record what you hear. Interact with it. This is a conversation starter, not a formula. Ticking the boxes and "completing the exercise" is not the goal. Conversing with the Lord and allowing Him to show you what He wants you to know is the goal.

chapter seven

THE HUMAN SPIRIT

"I long for You in the night; yes, my spirit within me diligently seeks You, for when Your judgments are in the land, the inhabitants of the world will learn righteousness"
(Isaiah 26:9, HCSB).

Journal Entry, 17th November, 2003: *" … see someone like Liv Tyler's character Arwen, in Lord of the Rings—sort of elfin-like, with shining, flowing robes and long curling hair…"*

Journal Entry, 20th November, 2003: *"…I went to my Boardroom before and asked You to come talk to my Heart…I asked if there were anyone else I should be inviting into the conversation, and You suggested my Spirit.*

"Now, I **had** *a picture of what I thought my Spirit looked like, but You said, "THAT'S NOT QUITE WHAT SHE LOOKS LIKE RIGHT NOW." …She has the potential to be what I imagined—to be that beautiful and stately being that commands respect—but the current reality is quite different!*

"I looked at the boardroom table and she was standing at the end—small, skinny, and homely—most likely undernourished. She was dirty and dressed in rags. I didn't even think to ask You **why** *she looked like that…"*

Meeting my Human Spirit was a shock and a challenge for me. How she looked certainly matched how I felt at the time, but I was prideful enough to want to reject the picture almost immediately. My rejection was not because I didn't think it was true and accurate, but because I knew it *was*. I just didn't want to admit it.

Proverbs 15:13 says, *"A joyful Heart makes a face cheerful, but a sad Heart produces a broken Spirit…"* *(HCSB, emphasis mine).* My husband has a phrase he often uses while preaching: "Sometimes *life* takes the life out of life!" We have come to understand this as meaning that sometimes the junk that happens to you has a paralyzing effect on the day-to-day. Being in ministry, we are exposed to *life* in this context to a greater degree than the average bear! Sometimes, it brings out the worst of us, stirring up junk that otherwise might go overlooked by us for most of our existence.

All this *life* takes its toll over time, making a Heart sad. Loss of loved ones, financial struggles, relational breakdowns, job concerns, conflicts between Believers, the basic *humanity* of the people we love and live and work with on a day-to-day basis, extracts a price. We are not impervious to the effects of other people's junk.

The more I learned about my Human Spirit, and the role God intended for it, the more apparent it became that I was very good at picking things up, but not so great at putting them down again! For instance—yes, I will go help that person. I will help carry that burden. The friend who discovered that their spouse was having an affair; the lady at church whose husband was dying; the man whose wife was chronically ill; the couple whose child was taken from them in an untimely manner and in the cruelest of ways; the young person who confides a secret sin to you; the older person who confides that they carry within their very being the consequences of a secret sin not dealt with; the family member who suffered at the hands of another; the child in your own house who was bullied at school; I will be there for them all. At some point, however, all of this humanness can cause a Heart to be sad and a Spirit to be broken.

No one person should ever have to deal with all this mess! Oh wait—I don't have to carry it alone. I forgot to put it down where it belongs—at the foot of the cross—because there *was* One who dealt with all of it already.

You see, what had happened with my Human Spirit was something that I am quite sure happens to everyone's Human Spirit at one time or another. *I took on more than I was supposed to.* In helping others, I picked up their junk and began to carry it as my own. I felt responsible.

My Human Spirit was starving for time with the Lord. If you remember, at the time I was learning about all this, I was coming out of the end of a very dry season with Him. I was overloading my Human Spirit with a bunch of stuff that she should never have had to deal with. Starving and neglected, my Human Spirit had no voice at the boardroom table and had lost the respect of the other members.

I may have been sweet-spirited, but I was a pushover! I had no spine, and could not stand up to anyone, for any reason. I didn't know how to say "no" to people, and I didn't know how to help someone without carrying more than I was meant to— "taking things personally," if you will. My hurting Heart and my out-of-control Emotions would take over and this sweet-spirited person would become mean and spiteful in a heartbeat, only to feel remorseful after the fact, thus heaping more unwanted junk on my Human Spirit.

The journey back to strength and wholeness is one that I am still traveling, and will most likely be traveling until I leave this earth to be with Jesus. For this reason, many of my insights and much of my understanding is still a work in progress. Understanding this, here is what I know of my Human Spirit. I know that my Human Spirit is designed to connect me with God. My Human Spirit is that part of me that will live forever—either with Him or separated from Him. God is eternal; I will merely continue to exist from this point on, into eternity. John 4:23-24 says, *"...An hour is coming, and is now here, when true worshippers will worship the Father in **spirit and in truth**. Yes, the Father wants such people to worship Him. **God is Spirit, and those who worship Him***

must worship in spirit and in truth" *(HCSB, emphasis mine).*

I know that my Human Spirit is *not* a wispy, misty, intangible puff of smoke. Neither is it a visible, but transparent, representation of my Body. Designed by God to exercise *dominion* in my boardroom, it must learn to work in partnership with the Holy Spirit; it is not meant to *dominate* in the boardroom or control the other members.

My Human Spirit, with the Holy Spirit, has just the right amount of strength, wisdom, and authority to lead the other board members wherever the Holy Spirit CEO desires and to do whatever He wills.

My Human Spirit needs time with the Lord—every day, not just once a week between ten and twelve o'clock on a Sunday morning. My Human Spirit is fed by His Word, and unlike my physical Body, gets hungrier the more it feeds. When my Human Spirit is healthy, it is what keeps my passion and desire for Him alive. If I neglect my Human Spirit, it gets weak and sickly and apathetic towards God and His ways.

Importantly, when my Human Spirit is weak and sickly, my Body tends to reflect that condition. We will explore that phenomenon in the next chapter, but for now, it is sufficient to note that the overall health of my Body is many times tied directly to the condition of my Human Spirit.

Keeping It Clean

Good spiritual hygiene is a concept I seemed quite oblivious to until a few years ago. Yes, I had been taught that 1 John 1:9 was "the Christian's bar of soap," and that I needed to have a daily "quiet time" with the Lord. I was taught, as I have said, to say my prayers every night before bed and to pray before every meal. Praying *for* people was something you promised to do during your quiet time, if you remembered, and was never something you talked too much about unless you wanted to be seen as prideful and self-important.

What I *found* was that living all of that out practically was a sure path to the weak, sickly, and apathetic lifestyle I was trying to dig myself out of, because it was not based on any kind of *relationship* with the Lord. I was just following a set of rules that I, and others, had laid out for me to follow.

I was reading through the Psalms one day while journaling and came to an awareness of something I hadn't seen before. All through the Psalms, the Psalmists command and exhort their readers to "Praise Him!", "Give thanks" to Him, "Put your faith/hope/trust" in Him. At no point, does it ever say in the Psalms "Do this when you *feel like* it," or "When the mood strikes you…", or "If you happen to think of it and no one is watching…"!

So often I let my Emotions dictate what I will or will not do—even though I know the purpose of my Emotions. If I'm happy, I will praise Him. If I'm in the mood, I will put on some worship music in the car. If I'm down, depressed, and out of sorts, then I don't feel like it and I'm not in the mood so I won't. The enemy knows that all he has to do is get me in the wrong mood and the praising stops; and then the mood darkens even more. Before I know it, weeks have gone by without significant fellowship with my Father. How frustrating that such a simple plan works so well—and how frustrating that I fall for it so often!

Praising God for who He is and for what He has done is as spiritually hygienic as brushing my teeth every day. Even if I'm tired, and I don't really feel like it, I could count on one hand the number of times I have *actually* missed cleaning my teeth over the years. Why? Because I know that if I *don't* brush my teeth, it will catch up to me eventually. Fuzzy, yellow teeth are unattractive, uncomfortable, and extremely off-putting, socially. Furthermore, my next trip to the dentist will see him poke a sharp pointy thing in the very place that will make me shout and jump and vow to *never again* miss a night of cleaning my teeth!

I have learned to clean my teeth *whether I feel like it or not*, because my Emotions don't get to have a say. People *notice* when I haven't cleaned my teeth, and I can't help wondering—if praising God is so important to my spiritual welfare and cleanliness, why don't I just *get it* and get *on* with *doing it*, already? One can't hide the consequences of not praising on a regular basis. Our spiritual breath gets stale and unpleasant, and no one wants to be around us when we're in that ungroomed state.

So—getting back to my introductory picture of my Human Spirit—it was all too obvious what the problem was, and all the other board members sent up a cry of defensive protest. Not one of them wanted to take any kind of responsibility for the state of my Human Spirit, even though it was brought to this state by the rules my Conscience had set, validated by my Mind and what I knew, and perpetuated by my Heart and Emotions because…well, because I didn't *feel* like it…

As it turned out, they were all rather suspicious of what my Spirit would do to them if she were healthy and powerful again; therefore, they were all quite happy to keep her in this weakened, neglected state.

Journal Entry, 20th November, 2003: *"I went into my boardroom before and asked You to come talk to my Heart. I asked if there were anyone else we should be inviting along—You suggested my Human Spirit… she came quietly, and when we came to the Heart she knelt down at the end of the bed (where the Heart was recovering) and hung her head. My Heart was cold—it showed no reaction to her. You asked my Heart if it would speak to us.*

H: "I want an apology!"

"FROM WHO?"

*H: "From **her**!" (Indicating my Human Spirit)*

"WHAT FOR?"

H: "She betrayed me!"

"There was no further explanation. My Human Spirit is still kneeling at the end of the bed, crying, and won't speak…"

My Heart had been offended because my Human Spirit would not listen to it. Bearing in mind, that this was the beginning of my journey,

I had a few things to sort out before my boardroom could function the way it was intended to function.

My Human Spirit's response to my Heart, up to that point, had been mostly, "*Really? I have to sit and listen to all that junk?*" Because of this hesitancy of my Human Spirit to want to listen, my Heart was somewhat justifiably upset and offended and was demanding an apology, if not an explanation, for being ignored for so long. Though malnourished, my Human Spirit was astute enough to realize the error she had made, and was more than willing to apologize and begin to do whatever it would take to strengthen herself and rebuild trust within the Boardroom.

Thou Shalt Learn to Love Me Again

This encounter with my Heart was a good start. One of the things to come out of all of this was that the Lord prescribed a daily diet for my Human Spirit that I was to follow without question. Basically, it entailed Bible reading, Bible reading, and more Bible reading. My initial reaction was a disheartened groan—I thought we had ditched all that legalism and rule following! "Thou shalt read thy Bible for 20 minutes every day!" However, what the Lord went on to describe to me was enlightening:

Journal Entry, Christmastime, 2007: "DEARHEART, I AM ASKING YOU TO TAKE A JOURNEY WITH ME—A HOLIDAY, OF SORTS. YOU ARE NOT READING TO GAIN KNOWLEDGE OR TO FULFILL A SCHEDULE OR TICK A BOX. YOU ARE ALLOWING YOUR HUMAN SPIRIT TO WALK WITH ME THROUGH THE PAGES, TO TAKE EVERYTHING IN, TO LOOK AT THE LANDSCAPE OF THE SCRIPTURES, AND TO BE REFRESHED, JUST BY HANGING OUT WITH ME IN MY SPACE.

"PRAISE AND WORSHIP ARE IMPORTANT, TOO, AND YOUR HUMAN SPIRIT WILL LEARN TO DO THAT MORE AND MORE AS YOU SPEND TIME IN MY WORD. LET HER HIDE IN ME FOR A SEASON, AND WHEN SHE IS STRENGTHENED, SHE WILL BE REVEALED AS THE ROYAL AND STATELY DAUGHTER YOU FIRST SAW!"

Consequently, for the course of a year, I read through the Bible. I found a reading plan that took me through the Old Testament once and the New Testament twice in that time, and I put no pressure on myself to journal every day, or to memorize verses, or anything of that nature. I just enjoyed the narrative and allowed the Holy Spirit CEO to impress on my Heart, Mind, and Human Spirit whatever He desired. I learned a lot and remembered a whole lot more than I thought I would during that time. My Human Spirit grew strong enough to step into her God-intended role of leadership in my boardroom.

Earlier, I mentioned that it is the Human Spirit's role to exercise dominion in the boardroom, in partnership with the Holy Spirit CEO, and not to dominate or control the other members. A good friend of mine, while sitting through this class on the Human Spirit, made this observation: "*Dominion* is based on mutual respect and love. *Domination* is based on fear and guilt." She couldn't have been more accurate.

The Holy Spirit—any member of the Godhead, for that matter—is a gentleman. He will not force, coerce, control, or make us do anything. To do so, would violate and render inactive our free will. Free will was the gift He gave us at the Creation of the world—it is the thing that makes us like Him—it is His image in us. He knew the ramifications of free will when He made us, and yet, He bestowed it upon us anyway. Free will is what makes our choice to follow Him, love Him, and live for Him a *choice—our* choice.

The Holy Spirit was sent at Pentecost to guide us into all truth, to comfort us and to nurture us in our faith and our walk with Him. He was not sent to dominate us and control us through fear, guilt, and shame. These are all ploys of the enemy to misdirect us and lead us awry. *Dominion* is His, now and forever—and the hallmark of dominion is mutual love and respect. We obey Him because we love Him. He guides, corrects, and disciplines us because He loves us. Our Human Spirit is meant to operate within our boardroom with the same mandate.

Wow—Look at Me Now!

Fast-forward a year, and my Human Spirit had learned to partner with the Holy Spirit CEO to help bring order to the boardroom. Just a reminder: By this stage in my walk, I had learned the sound of the various voices within my boardroom, as well as the voice of the Holy Spirit CEO, so the dialogue was flowing well in this encounter. I had learned, by this stage, that whenever dialogue happens between any board member, and myself it is actually my Human Spirit that initiates and perpetuates the conversation. When my Human Spirit speaks, I have denoted it with an "S." Allow me to share with you an example of my Human Spirit in action:

Journal Entry, 7th November, 2008: "*Yesterday **was** a bad day. Today I feel less anxious, but still pretty bad. A quick poll of my boardroom reveals that everyone is willing to work on whatever I need to work on. Except for the Heart. The Heart does not want to go there. She's just sitting at the table, stony-faced, with her hands spread on the table in front of her, shaking her head…*
S: "*Will you tell me why?*"
H: "*There's no point.*"
S: "*Why do you say that?*"
H: "*It won't get me anywhere.*"
S: "*What do you mean?*"

H: *"I'll drag out all my stuff, work it through, lots of pain…and then what? Someone else gets to come along and choose which scab to tear off next? This whole "turn the other cheek" business is fine unless you're the one who has to turn the other cheek."*

S: *"That's tough."*

H: *"Yeah."*

S: *"So what are you gonna do?"*

H: *"Sit here and protect my wounds."*

S: *"Okay…for how long?"*

H: *"For as long as it takes. Forever, maybe."*

S: *"That's a long time…So how are you going to stop others from coming in and hurting you again?"*

H: *"Same thing everyone else is doing. I'll just stop doing anything. I won't sing anymore. I won't lead anymore. I won't be hospitable. I'll go straight home after church so I don't have to talk to anyone…It seems to work for everyone else."*

S: *"It would be a pretty lonely existence though."*

H: *"No more so than I am now."*

S: *"Who are you trying to hurt by shutting down? God, or people?"*

H: *"I'm not **trying** to hurt anyone! I'm just aiming to protect myself."*

S: *"But you will hurt one of them, whether you're trying to or not…Is that what you want? To see people get hurt?"*

H: *"No! I just want them to stop hurting me…I feel taken for granted, used, and misunderstood. I feel mistreated…because people promise things they can't deliver, expect things from me I can't live up to, and take the liberty of correcting things in me that don't even need correcting…"*

S: *"And this is not the first time, is it?"*

H: *"No."*

S: *"Care to elaborate? It might help…"*

H: *"Help with what? No thanks…"*

S: *"You're being stubborn."*

H: *"Tell someone who cares!"*

S: *"Alright, I will. Lord Jesus, can I talk to you about my stubborn*

Heart?"

"OF COURSE..."

S: "Lord, she's so hurt and bruised—she won't talk, and I'm stuck. We need to move on from here, but she won't budge..."

"SHE NEEDS YOU TO LISTEN."

S: "I **want** to listen, but she won't **say** anything!"

"LISTEN TO HER SILENCE. LISTEN TO WHAT SHE'S **NOT** SAYING. FEEL HER PAIN. **LISTEN TO HER SILENCE...**"

S: "She's not stubborn; she's paralyzed—held captive by fear."

"GOOD! WHAT ELSE?"

S: "Self-righteousness and pride...didn't she get rid of these earlier?"

"SHE CHALLENGED THE BELIEF; NOW IT IS TIME TO WEED OUT THE PEDDLERS OF THAT BELIEF."

S: "But she'll not agree to that"

"SHE DOESN'T HAVE TO."

S: "But You're a gentleman—how will You get rid of them if she won't agree?"

"NOT ME, YOU. YOU HAVE THE RIGHT TO FIGHT FOR HER. THE HUMAN SPIRIT (THAT'S YOU) COMMUNICATES WITH THE HOLY SPIRIT (THAT'S ME) AND THEY WORK TOGETHER TO BRING ORDER TO THE BOARDROOM. YOUR JOB IS TO HELP HER GET TO THE POINT OF BEING WILLING TO HEAR FROM ME. THAT MEANS THAT SOMETIMES YOU WILL HAVE TO FIGHT FOR HER."

S: "Wow. Okay, so what do I do?"

"BIND THEM."

S: "Can't I just cast them out?"

"YOU BIND THEM. SHE CASTS THEM OUT."

S: "Alright. Fear, pride, and self-righteousness—in the name of Jesus Christ I bind you and command you to let go of my Heart! (Was that okay?)"

"YES DEARHEART, NOW CONTINUE..."

H: "What did you just do?"

S: *"Only what He told me to do—bound that which was holding you and released you from it..."*

The conversation I had goes on for many pages more, as my Heart begins conversing directly with the Lord about the effects that fear and pride had in my life at that time. The point of all this—my Human Spirit did the job she was designed to do; she brought my Heart to the point of being able to talk with, and hear from, Jesus.

THE THIEF CAME TO STEAL, KILL, AND DESTROY

The advent of the New Age Movement in the 1960s and 1970's triggered a powerful response from the conservative church. In my (albeit, limited) observation, the Human Spirit was banished; relegated to the basement of theological thinking and was spurned as being a part of ourselves that could be overindulged and spoiled, and therefore, not trusted.

Because of the very real damage that Transcendental Meditation and imaginative meetings with demonic spirit guides has done to humanity, anyone who paid any kind of attention to the Human Spirit—their own or anyone else's—was looked upon as strange, weird, or severely deceived. Any encouragement to *feed* our Human Spirit was looked upon with equal suspicion. Holistic Health (Mind, Body, Spirit), and all it espoused, was rejected as a tool of the devil.

Consequently, the Human Spirit, in many Christian circles, was deliberately ignored. I believe this is to our detriment. As a follower of Christ, I must worship Him *in spirit and in truth*. How do I engage my Human Spirit in worship of God if my Human Spirit has been neglected?

There is a truth that is widely accepted across all denominations, and that is that humanity is designed to worship. If we do not worship God, then we *will* worship something else. This is how the enemy got so much traction with the New Age Movement—he capitalized on our tendency to worship the *something else* and exploited it. Unfortunately, as we came out the other side of that movement, what we were left with is a twisted and corrupted view of spirituality that only allows room for suspicion and avoidance of anything that might *accidentally* draw us into the counterfeit world that the enemy has built.

Frank Perretti, in his books, "This Present Darkness" and "Piercing the Darkness", brought this world vividly to life for Christians, who were skeptical about the reality of such a spirit-world, yet were strangely drawn to the concepts Perretti introduced. I remember reading these books in my teen years, with the caution to "not take them too seriously!"; but Perretti's message spoke to me, stirring my imagination in a way that I had not previously allowed it to be stirred. He opened up to me the idea that the spiritual realm was, indeed, real—not just a concept used by the church to explain how salvation and prayer worked.

Flights of Fancy?

If you'll recall, in the chapter on the Mind, I suggested that the Mind was the interface between the physical realm that we exist in and the spiritual realm. At this point, it is worth mentioning that the Mind is also the seat of our *imagination*. Many of us have squashed this God-given ability in the name of righteousness, thinking that our imagination is just a pathway that the enemy uses to distort and pervert our thought life. While this can be true, we have to remember that it is also true that the enemy can *only* pervert or distort something that was already created, because he does not have the ability to create anything.

Let me explain what I mean by that statement. When God made man in His own image, He said that it was good. There is no one in all eternity who has an imagination like God! To imagine something is to create it in your Mind, to see, conjure, or dream up things that were not previously there.

As humans, when we imagine, we create from what is already known. We take an already created concept or reality and work with it in our Mind to change it in some way. When *God* imagined, He created a universe, planets, plants, animals, and people from *nothing*! Everything that you see in this world was created in the Mind of God before it came into being in our reality.

The enemy has the same ability we have—we can take what God created and pervert, distort, destroy, or corrupt it, but we cannot make something out of nothing. We can also take what God has given us and learn to use it the way He intended—to draw us closer to Himself. Everything He created was for our benefit and our pleasure…until the fall of mankind. At that point, our imagination, along with everything else, became subject to the enemy's schemes.

Our imagination is one function of our Mind that we need to learn to restore and redeem. If the enemy can use our imagination to destroy us, then *surely* it is true that God can use it to communicate with us and draw us closer to His heart. At risk of overstating the point—the enemy can only counterfeit what is already there. Has humanity been corrupted through the enemy's distortion of the imagination? Undoubtedly, yes; but to dismiss the imagination as unnecessary or useless is a grave mistake and one that costs us dearly.

Practically everything that we do in life requires that we use our imagination to some extent. Science, medicine, inventions, entertainment, architecture, research, forensic anthropology, landscaping, graphic design, accounting, or rearranging the lounge room furniture…literally, *anything* you can think of that man puts his Mind and his hand to do requires, in some capacity, the use of imagination.

Thinking outside the box. Pushing the boundaries. Exploring new ways and means of achieving results. If you've ever asked the question, "What if…?", then you have used your imagination. If you have ever watched a television show or a movie, you have engaged your imagination. You have suspended belief long enough to immerse yourself in a story outside of yourself to live vicariously through the characters you see on the screen in front of you.

Every person has the God-given capacity to engage the imagination in conversation with God. Let me be clear—I am *not* saying that we should imagine what we would want God to say and, in this way, make up or invent a conversation with God. That would create a closed system in which we could make God be whoever we wanted Him to be and say whatever we wanted Him to say. God is not someone we can jam into a box or contain in such a way. That's how the enemy hijacked what God intended for good and twisted it to give rise to New Age.

Rather, I *am* saying that God can use and direct our imagination to reveal Himself to us. He can reveal things about our areas of weakness and growth (called *revelation*) that we, otherwise, would not have visited.

1 John 2:27, the Good News Bible says, *"But as for you, Christ poured out His Spirit on you. As long as His Spirit remains in you, you do not need anyone to teach you. For His Spirit teaches you about everything, and what He teaches is true, not false. Obey the Spirit's teaching then, and remain in union with Christ."* Consequently, it is in *this* realm—the spiritual realm, and the imaginative realm—that our Human Spirit steps into its God-given authority and mandate to worship God in spirit and in truth, and to connect the rest of the boardroom to God.

Romans 8:16 says, *"The Spirit Himself **testifies together with our** [human] **spirit** that we are God's children…"* (HCSB, emphasis and extra brackets mine). Similarly, 1 John 3:24 says, *"The one who keeps His commands remains in Him, and He in him. And **the way that we know that He remains in us is from the Spirit He has given us**"* (HCSB, emphasis mine). Again, in 1 John 4:13, he says, *"**This is how we know** we remain in Him, and He in us. He has given assurance to us **from His Spirit**"* (HCSB, emphasis mine). The gift of our Human Spirit is what enables us to hear from the Holy Spirit CEO.

If you are having trouble wrapping your head around all of this, and want a Biblical example of how the Human Spirit connects with God on a spiritual/imaginative level, spend some time in the books of Daniel, Ezekiel, parts of Isaiah (chapter six in particular) and Revelation. All of these describe being "taken up in the Spirit" and seeing things not of this world.

Whenever any of the prophets say that, "The Spirit of the Lord came upon me," they are describing a spiritual encounter with God, which was even more significant in the Old Testament because these men had not received the Holy Spirit in the same way that the early Christians had. For the prophets of old, to have the Spirit of the Lord come upon them was a weighty responsibility, indeed, and a lonely path to walk because there were very few others who could relate to the things they were seeing and feeling.

Ezekiel's vision by the Chebar Canal was an imaginatively spiritual encounter, in the sense that God engaged his imagination in order to show him the things He wanted to reveal. In the same way, John's vision in Revelation was given through the Holy Spirit, whom John received at Pentecost, and the Holy Spirit engaged John's imagination in order to show him what was to happen in the end times.

The reason we find visions, dreams, and spiritual pictures so hard to accept is because the enemy has corrupted something that God intended for our good. Staying away from the original does not make the counterfeit less powerful, it actually makes the counterfeit *more* powerful, because now we can't, or won't, even access the original, or gain any benefit from its existence for fear of becoming entangled in the counterfeit.

Let me ask you this question: How does a bank clerk know if a dollar bill is an original or a counterfeit? They do not spend time studying counterfeit bills. They spend time studying and working with the real deal. As they are consistently exposed to the real thing, they will immediately know something is not right when the counterfeit finds its way into their hands. They feel it in the texture of the paper or the texture of the ink.

When I trained as a midwife, one of the tasks we were given was *abdominal palpation* or to feel a woman's pregnant belly. We were given a very particular set of instructions and a comprehensive list of the things we were to look for in the examination. Every time we saw a pregnant woman in the clinic or hospital, one of the examinations we performed was an abdominal palpation, along with the usual temperature, pulse, and blood pressure.

The more pregnant bellies we felt, the more familiar we became with the feel of the baby through the layers of the woman's stomach. We performed this examination to establish the position of the baby prior to birth. The optimal position for labor and birth is for the baby to be head down, and facing the mother's right hip. We all got to the stage in our training where, within seconds of placing our hands on a woman's belly, we could say with a high measure of accuracy which side the baby was facing, and that the baby was, indeed, head down.

One day, as I was performing this examination, I picked up that something was not right with the position of the baby *within seconds* of placing my hands on the woman's abdomen. How could I be so sure? Because *I was so familiar with what was normal*, or right. I knew instantly that this baby was breech or feet down. As a result of my findings, an ultrasound was ordered. The baby's position was verified, and steps were then taken to correct the position of the baby prior to birth.

If we spend regular, intentional time in the Word of God, allowing our Human Spirit to *hang out* with Jesus in His natural territory, over time we gain the ability to discern very quickly what is right and what is not, or what is of God and what is the enemy. Spending time in the Word regularly means that I get to know the sound and the feel of God's voice. I get to know the tones and inflections of His voice, how He sounds, the sorts of things He says, and the sorts of things He would *never* say. This is how I know I can trust where He leads me, and how I know I am following the Holy Spirit CEO—because *I know the voice of my Shepherd*; this is the job that my Human Spirit was created to do.

Now It's Your Turn

Once the Human Spirit has learned to know the voice of the Lord and it has made the connection with God, its job in the boardroom is to step out of the way and facilitate the conversation between the Holy Spirit CEO and the other board members.

The Human Spirit will always be present; it doesn't hide or abdicate its authority or its job to the other board members, it remains present, much like a Personal Assistant to the CEO of a large company. The Personal Assistant is the one who sets up the meetings and ensures that the people required in attendance at those meetings are prepared, equipped, and in the right place at the right time. The Personal Assistant is the one who handles the correspondence. He/she is aware of any tensions, knows the names of each board member's spouses and children, and is able to connect with them all on a personal level—but once that person has been delivered to the meeting, the Personal Assistant steps aside. Still working behind the scenes, their presence is no longer noticed.

In like fashion, the Human Spirit will be aware of the underlying tensions in the boardroom and help pinpoint which member is having trouble submitting to the Holy Spirit CEO. The Human Spirit will get alongside that board member to have the conversation that is necessary to bring that member to a place of being willing to talk to the Holy Spirit CEO about whatever their issue may be. Then it steps aside, again.

You could also think of the Human Spirit as being like a power cord that plugs into the power outlet in order to turn on the lamp. The lamp will never give light if the cord is not plugged in. Once the cord is connected to the power outlet, it goes pretty much unnoticed because the lamp is giving the light it was made to give. We only notice the cord if it becomes disconnected from the outlet for any reason. In the same way, the Human Spirit connects us to God. Once that outcome has been achieved, the Human Spirit goes mostly unnoticed…unless it becomes disconnected for any reason. When the lamp doesn't work, the first thing we check is whether or not it's plugged into the power source. When we feel disconnected, our Human Spirit is the first place we should be checking.

Are you connected to God? If you are, it's a great place to begin this session with Him. Praise Him. Adore Him. Worship Him. If not, ask Him what you need to do to get reconnected.

Ask Him, "How do You see my Human Spirit? What state is he/she in?" What does the Lord say about your Human Spirit's health? He loves to discuss these things with you, and you will be pleasantly surprised by some of His answers! The journey is always fun, and the conversation intriguing,, so go talk…He's waiting for you.

chapter eight

THE BODY

"Dear friend, I pray that you may prosper in every way and be in good health physically just as you are spiritually"
(3 John, verse 2, HCSB).

Journal Entry, 3rd February, 2004: *"... My Body is straining under some kind of weight—I can't see what..."*

Journal Entry, 8th May, 2007: *"...My body is tied to a chair—arms, legs, chest—ropes everywhere, so that every movement hurts..."*

Journal Entry, 13th May, 2007: *"...Okay—so now it's bending over backwards. Before it was tied to a chair...I'm bending over backwards to keep everyone happy, but it's not working...Is this why my back is so sore?"*

In February of 2004, I had my first—and thankfully, my *only*—bout of kidney stones. I was attending Thursday Group and felt a little gripey, so I took myself off to the bathroom. Locked in the cubicle of the ladies' room, I remember a few moments of overwhelming pain, during which I heard the Lord say, "You're going to be okay. Nothing's going to happen to you that I don't already know about. I've got you!"

I thought I had only been gone a few minutes, but when I returned to the group, I was met with a few concerned glances. I discovered later that I been gone almost a half-hour. I indicated that I would prefer to stand while the group continued, and a short while later found myself surrounded by women as I doubled over with another wave of excruciating pain.

The group discussion discontinued and people gathered around—laying me down, making me comfortable, praying for me, asking relevant (and not so relevant) questions. I heard someone call for an ambulance. The dear lady cradling my head began "praying in the Spirit"—a concept I was not at all familiar with at that point in my journey—and she was shaking violently. I do remember telling her I didn't mind the praying, but would God mind terribly if she stopped shaking my head?

Throughout the whole ordeal, I was very aware of the Presence of God and His peace. While I was dealing with the very worst pain I think I have ever had in my life, His peace enveloped me *totally*. Many of the women present reported that I smiled a lot and was *so* peaceful.

The ambulance arrived in due course, and I was given some pain relief and taken off to the hospital, amidst reassurances from friends that they would call Mark and organize to pick the kids up from school. I spent a few hours in the ER, and then was sent home, only to return in the early morning hours when the symptoms returned with a vengeance. Diagnosis took some time but, once they were certain it was kidney stones, I was transferred by ambulance to another campus of the hospital, where I settled in to wait for it to pass.

I was super nauseated from all the morphine that had been pumped into my Body, which was the only thing that would control the pain, and at this campus, the policy was that morphine was to be administered no more than once every four hours. They did not have standing orders; the doctor had to be called each time it was required, to give authorization for another dose. As it had been less than two hours since my last dose, the nurse was unyielding to Mark's request that she call the doctor. Her boundary was solid and her response seemed practiced—"I'm sorry. I know it's uncomfortable, but it's not time yet."

I was far too preoccupied with the searing hot poker in my back to even try to make sense of the policy, or the nurse's cracked-record response. I remember very little of that day; I saw Mark's worried face looking down at me from the end of a very long tunnel; my Body was so braced against the pain I'm sure my tight grip left an indentation in the bedrail.

I vaguely recall snippets of conversation between an angry sounding doctor, my husband close to tears, and the nurse who was told to "prep her for surgery *now*!" I saw my friend, Amie, as they wheeled me out of the room. The next thing I was aware of was the doctor, still in his scrubs, mask hanging under his triumphant grin, as he shook the offending kidney stone in a small plastic specimen jar.

"*That* thing was *never* gonna pass!" he announced with pride—as if I had just given birth to a fifteen-pound baby. "It's *huge*!"

My recovery from that little incident was long and arduous. Many weeks would pass before the morphine cleared out of my system and I no longer felt nauseated. That kidney stone left a legacy of an aching and spasming back that lasted for almost a decade. I could not sleep lying down. I would wake up at around three or four every morning, unable to move. Just rolling over in bed was an ordeal.

My hips, my lower back, and my sides would burn and ache. I discovered that the pain was less intense if I sat up in a recliner chair, or propped myself up on pillows to sleep, but I still required heat packs or ice packs in the early hours of the morning to help alleviate the pain and ease the ache. I needed Mark to help me get out of bed in the mornings.

I went to a physiotherapist, took up Pilates, visited a myotherapist, massage therapists, a chiropractor or two, and even went so far as to have prayer for healing on numerous occasions. During the day, once I got moving, there was no issue—pain-free and mobile I could still function, but the night times were a different story. I dreaded going to bed.

It's All Connected

Our Body lives out physically what our board members wrestle with internally. Sure, there were physical factors in the contraction of the kidney stones in the first place. I didn't drink enough water and probably ate too much of the wrong kinds of foods. Truth be told, I didn't really look after my Body very well at all in those days.

Around the same time, I was also struggling with Irritable Bowel Syndrome (IBS), something that I had been told I would have to live with for the rest of my life because there was no cure. On the upside, those who suffered from IBS rarely had any problems with bowel cancer. Oh good. That's an *awesome* upside! The *downside* was that I spent a good deal of time bloated, crampy, nauseated and…well, it's not really polite to talk about it in mixed company, and I'm sure you get the picture.

All that to say, the Lord had already been challenging me on some of my dietary habits, so I was going through an intensely focused awareness of what was good for my Body and what was not. I was also learning how to identify within myself which board members were causing trouble and why. Sometimes we need the benefit of distance to be able to see how we are being disciplined and trained.

I began to learn that the messages my Heart was sending me, in the form of Emotions, had a direct correlation to what my Body was feeling at any given moment. For example—I felt anxiety as a knot in my stomach. I felt agitation and frustration as tightness in my neck and shoulders. I felt stress and tension as a headache and, in the aftermath of any kind of spiritual breakthrough, (which I then referred to as *heart work*), I felt an intense migraine like pain behind my right eye.

Why do I make that connection? Mostly because I learned to pay attention, but also because the more I talked to the Lord about it all, the more He *told* me it was connected. I learned that my Heart actually *liked* being sick—not how it felt to be sick, exactly, but it liked the attention it got when I was sick. My dad is a medical doctor—a family physician—so growing up with an authority on *sick* had its perks… but mostly it was just aggravating! He could always tell if I was faking so I rarely got away with skipping school because of illness. My friends would tell me how fun it was to "chuck a sickie," (meaning pretending to be ill so they could stay home from school). I never knew the pleasure (*sighs*). My Heart recognized that if I was *really* sick, I got the attention I thought I wanted. If my recovery was slow, I got prolonged sympathy.

Does this mean that illness is all in my head? No, not at all. What it means is that once I learned to deal with the Heart issue of wanting attention, there was no longer any benefit to remaining ill. After the kidney stones, my recovery improved significantly once I was able to determine what it was that my Heart wanted, because being sick wasn't what got me what I needed.

Going to the Lord was the only way I could get what I needed and, once that was recognized, my focus was able to shift from getting what I wanted from being sick to getting what I needed from *Him*. Everything else just kind of fell into place.

It's Not You, It's Me

So, what does this all mean?

I am pleased to report to you that at the time of this writing, my back is healed. I am pain-free at nighttime and I have been for the past four years. I can sleep lying down, all night, and am not awakened by aching hips. I am also free from any symptoms of IBS. Why? Because God is just *that* good! Also, because I was able to take my physical ailments to Him and hear what He had to say about the way I treated my Body.

My healing did not happen instantly. That's not to say that I don't think that God can heal instantly, because I firmly believe that He can and does—but for me it took time. The Lord put me on a learning curve, and I'm sad to have to admit that I'm a really slow learner in some instances. Sometimes the delay in our healing is because of *us*, not because of *Him*.

I started to take an interest in what I fed my Body, and learned that some foods had an adverse effect on my Body and its functions. I learned that every Body is different in its responses to those foods.

For example, my husband and my kids could all eat wheat with no problem, but my gut reacted violently to anything derived from wheat. Australia is a wheat-growing nation, so many of the additives in preserved and packaged foods were derived from wheat because it was readily available and relatively inexpensive. Sweeteners, thickeners, and colorings that were derived from some part of wheat processing were laced throughout most of the foods that I had considered a staple in my family's diet, and I was shocked at the amount of foods that had wheat in them.

Ice cream, for instance, was mostly sweetened with wheat glucose syrup. There was one brand and two flavors that I could safely enjoy. Many of the candy bars in Australia were sweetened with wheat glucose syrup. Cough lollies and throat lozenges fell into that same category. Many medications had wheat listed among the non-active ingredients as binders or thickeners.

A whole new (and tediously laborious) way of food gathering opened itself up to me as I found myself reading labels and investigating the contents of everything I consumed. I began buying ingredients separately and making my own food from scratch, instead of purchasing things premade, because then I could monitor what was in the food I ate.

The process of changing my lifestyle was a long one…and I had an open-ended and ongoing conversation with the Lord about it for many years. I became so focused on treating my Body right that I lost sight of my Body! Listen to this conversation between my Human Spirit, my

Body, and the Lord.

> ***Journal Entry, 13th May, 2007:*** *S: "Why does my back still hurt?"*
> *"TAKE A LOOK AT YOUR BODY."*
> *S: "Okay—it's bending over backwards. Before, it was tied to a chair. Why is it doing that?*
> *"ASK IT."*
> *S: "Body, what are you doing?"*
> *B: "What's expected of me?"*
> *S: "What do you mean? Who expects you to bend over backwards?"*
> *B: "All the others."*
> *S: "How do you know?"*
> *B: "Guilt is thrown at me by the Emotions because the Heart wants me to do things I don't feel I can do. The Mind is too overloaded to pay much attention anymore. The Will thinks it's on my side, but most of the time I feel it's working against me. **You** ignore me—that's probably why Jesus doesn't fix me."*
> *S: "Wow. Pretty convincing—but why do you think I ignore you?"*
> *B: "Because Jesus doesn't heal me. You're the one who's supposed to communicate with Him, but you never tell Him about me."*
> *S: "I **do** tell Him about you…!"*
> *B: "No, you don't. The Heart complains about me to Him, but you don't pray for me like you do for the others. You lead the Heart to Him, the Heart complains, but nothing changes. I'm bending over backwards to keep everyone in here happy, but it's not working and everyone has their own solution for me. Jesus talks to everyone in here, but you don't ever lead me to Him to talk. I want to talk to Him and not have everyone else do it on my behalf! I'm so tired right now—I need to sleep. And it's pointless trying to keep me awake, because I need sleep, and I can and will shut everyone down in order to get it…everyone in here benefits if I'm well rested and taken care of!"*
> *S: "Fair point. Can we finish this tomorrow?"*
> *B: "**If** I have time. You know—gym, lunch dates, chiropractor, violin*

lessons, life group—you need me to get you to all of those things, you do realize this, don't you?'"

That my Body would want its own audience with the Lord was a fascinating revelation to me. More than that, I was feeling chastised—by my own Body! I wrote in my journal as a follow-up the next day, *"…basically, I think my Body longs to be renewed, but the other board members just want the new Body without the process; to let this one return to the dust it came from. While it is true that this is the Body that You have given me; this is the house for my Human Spirit **and** Yours, and I feel I am learning to accept it as it is…I don't want my Body "bending over backwards" to keep the boardroom happy!"*

In due course, I came to understand what the Lord had been telling me; that *everything is connected*; that the choices I make, or don't make, have a direct or an indirect effect on my physical well-being. I eventually got to a stage where I realized that my Body was craving attention that my Mind had judged as being wrong or ungodly. We touched on the topic of counterfeits and the New Age Movement in the last chapter, but let me explain further.

But I Came so That You May Have Life

There has been a move in the last couple of decades toward "total wellness," or "holistic health," meaning wellness of the whole. Mind, Body, Spirit conferences have been run in New Age circles for years; being *present* in the moment, or being *mindful* of ourselves and our surroundings and circumstances in any given moment has fast become popular in our society. "Only when we are addressing the health needs of the *whole* Body, can we *truly be* healthy." If we remember that *truth is still truth, no matter who lays claim to it,* we can agree that there is truth in that statement.

Within the church circles where I grew up, these kinds of approaches to health and wellness were avoided because they all encompassed some form of ungodly, unbiblical, un*christian* philosophy that was not just displeasing to God, but was also intrinsically harmful to the Believer. Rather than be deceived, it was better to "suffer with Jesus" and humbly learn whatever lesson He had for us in the circumstance.

I don't write this with any sense of mockery or scorn. On the contrary, it's *truth*, and I fully respect and accept it as such. In the past, though, when it came to ascertaining truth in those practices, I (like many others) have tossed the baby out with the bathwater.

John 10:10 says, *"A thief comes to steal and to kill and to destroy. I have come so that they may have life, and* **have it in abundance***" (HCSB, emphasis mine)*. This means that anything God ever said was good—anything God ever said at all, actually—will be twisted and perverted by the enemy in order to mislead and destroy us.

In John 14:6, Jesus says, *"I am the Way, the* **Truth** *and the Life. No one comes to the Father except through me" (HCSB, emphasis mine)*. If Jesus is Truth, then all truth belongs to Him. Something cannot be true, or truth, and not be of God. Even the devil knows this, so he poisons truth with a lie. Sadly, for most of my life, I allowed the lie to poison the truth and, therefore, discarded a lot of truth *as* a lie.

Let's take Yoga, for example; the *religion* of Yoga, or the *spiritual practice* of Yoga is steeped in Eastern Mysticism and questionable spiritual beliefs. The spiritual practice of Yoga is a slippery beast to pin down. If you Google "Yoga," you will scroll through pages of many and varied forms of Yoga…all quite overwhelming and mind-boggling. You don't have to scratch too far beneath the surface to discover that no matter what type of Yoga you find and practice, there is one thing they all have in common—the physical exercises and poses are all tied to various spiritual beliefs and practices. As the devotee practices these exercises, the Yoga instructor encourages them to focus their thoughts on the spiritual beliefs that go with the particular exercise.

There have been many who could testify to being drawn into the spiritual practices of Yoga after simply exploring the physical aspect of the discipline. On the flip side, there are probably just as many who never even knew there *was* a spiritual aspect to Yoga. The question remains; are the physical benefits of Yoga negated by the fact that there is a counterfeit spiritual practice associated with it? If doing the physical exercises helps to strengthen the Body, release stress and tension, and make it more flexible, why does it work? Yoga works because of the physical truth and not because of the counterfeit spiritual practices.

If I avoid Yoga, and anything that resembles Yoga because of the counterfeit spiritual practice (in case I get drawn into a lie of the enemy), then I must also avoid any kind of stress-relieving stretching and relaxation exercise, because most of it is derived in some way from the physical practice of Yoga. Furthermore, if I avoid stress-relieving exercise, then my Body learns to deal with stress by holding onto it, internalizing it, and carrying it around.

Like the children of Israel before us, we who are God's children should be able to demonstrate a level of health and wellbeing in our Bodies that is a living, walking testimony to His goodness. Instead, many people look at Christians and wonder why we would choose to embrace sickness and chronic pain, rather than embrace a method of exercise that could help us.

As I have previously mentioned, my dad is a family physician or general practitioner, if you're Aussie. My husband, Mark, recalls a conversation with my dad, years ago, where Mark asked him, "How much of people's illnesses are stress-related?" Dad's answer was telling. He said that about *eighty percent* of illnesses, in his estimation, were stress-related, or in some other way related to what people think and how they deal with stress. That's not to say that most people's sickness is all in their heads, but rather, those who deal with stress appropriately spend far less time in the doctor's office than those who don't.

You see, if someone practices Yoga and is healthy and stress free because of it, I would suggest that it is because of the *truth* that the physical exercise associated with Yoga helps relieve stress and tension in the Body, thus giving the Body a chance to recover and *be* healthy, not because of the *counterfeit* spirituality that goes with it. The physical exercise and practice of Yoga is merely an example of God's principles of truth working in spite of the corruption or misinformation that surrounds it.

Read Psalm 73 when you have a spare moment or two, and see how the Psalmist wrestles with the conundrum that presents itself when truth works despite corruption. He is acutely aware of the fact that the wicked seem to prosper while those whose hearts are pure suffer and struggle. If the wicked man follows principles that God, Himself, set in place to ensure our well-being and prosperity, then he *will* prosper, for truth does not stop being truth simply because someone twists it for their own purposes. If that were the case, God and truth would cease to exist.

By the end of Psalm 73, the Psalmist comes to the realization that, although the wicked man may *appear* to prosper in this life, he does so at the expense of his eternal soul because, *"Those far from [God] will certainly perish, for [He] destroy[s] all those who are unfaithful to [Him]"* (Psalm 73:27, HCSB, extra brackets mine).

I mention this because there were many who were concerned for my well-being as I journeyed with the Lord through this process. These people expressed concern that I would be deceived along the way by accepting treatment for my back that was not exactly kosher, you might say. My answer to those concerns is this: If the enemy came to steal, kill, and destroy, and his M.O. is to drive me further away from the Heart of God, then anything that draws me closer to His Heart and deeper into relationship with Him *cannot* be from the enemy. A house divided against itself will not stand. Therefore, for the enemy to try to ensnare me by causing me to run *to* the very one he wants me to have no part in, makes no tactical sense any way you slice it.

I am closer to God, and He gets all the Glory for my healed state. That is a clear win for the good guys, and a devastating loss for the enemy.

Tune In

So, how does one begin to hear from their Body? I'm so glad you asked! There are a few things you can do to get started. Becoming aware of the Body's messages takes time and practice, and if we have practiced *ignoring* the Body's messages for any length of time, we may have lost touch with the health issues we need to address.

Physical pain is a message that something is wrong. A good deal of the aches and pains that we feel on a daily basis as we get older are dismissed as being a normal part of the aging process, but God did not design us to become old before our time! Sadly, that is of our own doing.

To this end, the sensations we experience through our Body are meant to make us aware of what is going on, not just in our Body, but also in our inner world. Many times, there is a huge divide between what we are thinking and how our Body is reacting to life.

I regularly visit a personal trainer—a Christian gentleman in his early sixties. To look at him, you would not think him a day over forty. Each week, as I enter the studio, he looks at me and asks the inevitable question, "How is your Body?" The funny thing is we both know that I don't even need to answer him, because he can tell *me* how my Body is better than I can, just by looking at me. I try and answer anyway, because it makes me have to tune in to what my Body is telling me.

Almost from my first visit with him, he began telling me, "Everything is connected!" This was no coincidence, and I soon understood that just as everything is connected internally, everything is connected physically, as well, in ways that were quite surprising. If I walk in with tightness in my neck and shoulders, Calvin will often start working on my feet and calves. Why? Because everything is connected. If I am tight in my calves, it's because of a problem in my feet. My hamstrings won't release if my calves are tight, and in turn, my hips and lower back won't release if my hamstrings and quads are tight. In order to loosen my neck and shoulders—where I am *feeling* the tightness and pain—we have to target another area first. That way, when release comes, it *stays*.

Calvin often prays over me as he works, and I have learned not to be surprised that when I am particularly tight or sore in an area that won't release easily, the Lord will show me an area in my boardroom that requires attention. For example, my Heart may be stubbornly holding onto an idea or a belief that it doesn't want to let go of.

As he works on me, Calvin will pray for release; he often just says the word "release!" as he massages and stretches the muscle. The physical sensation is painful, because he's working on areas of my Body that are sore, but when the release comes it is more than just a physical release. I now understand that *how my Body is feeling*—how it behaves and responds—is connected to *what's going on inside of me*. On more than one occasion, there have been tears on my part as emotional, spiritual, *and* physical release all coincide. I leave with enough energy to take on the world, but feeling like I could just as easily curl up and take a nap, simultaneously.

The Bible tells us that the Body is the temple, or the sanctuary, of the Holy Spirit CEO (See 1 Corinthians 6:19-20). The apostle Paul also tells us to "*...give your bodies to God because of all He has done for you. Let them be a living and Holy sacrifice—the kind He will find acceptable. This is truly the way to worship Him*" (Romans 12:1, NLT). In the Old Testament, only an unblemished animal would be acceptable as a sacrifice to the Lord. Here Paul tells us to give our Bodies as a sacrifice to God—but the way we treat our Bodies often renders them *unacceptable* as a sacrifice to God because, as a result of our mistreatment, we drag around extra weight, stress, pain, and conditions of illness that could be looked at as *blemishes*.

I'm not talking about the pimples on your forehead, or the size of your nose, or anything cosmetic that comes with the package of *you*, and I do recognize that there are some illnesses that do not fall into this category. I'm talking about the things we *could* do something about, if all our board members were submitted to the Holy Spirit CEO, but *won't* because we'd rather do things our own way.

When I was told I had IBS, and that it would most likely be with me forever, I saw an endless future of tummy aches and lethargy and bloatedness. Then God showed me some things I could change. I had a choice. There were a number of things I had to give up in order to gain a healthier gut. Some of those things were easy to give up, but others—not so much! Like meat pies and sausage rolls, hot jam donuts, funnel cakes, poffertjes, and lamingtons…if I sat here and thought hard enough I could depress myself with the long list of things I miss out on. (To this day, I have never tasted a Krispy Kreme donut, and most likely never will 'cause it just isn't worth the hours of suffering!)

Instead, I look at the things I have gained. I am no longer bloated and lethargic. I have more energy. I stay healthier, and I really don't miss out on much at all. The living sacrifice I am able to make, daily, is my choice to lay aside the temporary pleasures of wheat-infused yumminess in order to take hold of the eternal pleasure of treating my Body and living the way God planned—for His Glory.

Now It's Your Turn

As always, begin with adoration, praise, and worship. Thank Him for the gift of your Body. Take a few moments to become aware of His presence with you. Also, take notice of what your Body is telling you at this moment. Where are you sitting? Are you comfortable? Are you at a desk or curled on a sofa?

Close your eyes, if you like, and pay attention to every area of your Body, from the top of your head to the tips of your toes and everything else in between. Notice the areas that are tight or sore. Is your head feeling achy? Are your shoulders relaxed? As I type, I am noticing my own eyes are little tired, and I feel a headache coming on from the tightness that is building between my shoulder blades…ironic that I have been so engrossed in the typing of this topic that I have forgotten to pay attention to the messages my own Body is sending me.

As you hear the messages from your Body, write these down on a piece of paper or in your journal. You can draw a rough gingerbread man shape to represent your Body, and mark on this any areas of pain, discomfort, tightness, or tension. You can use different colored pens or markers to indicate the things that need urgent attention, or attention sometime in the near future, or other things that you just need to keep an eye on. Use this as a springboard for discussion with the Lord about any stress you are carrying or health needs of immediate concern. Ask Him how He sees your Body and how He would want *you* to see your Body. Allow Him to talk to you about your Body's limitations.

For example, if you know that by five p.m. *every* Friday evening you have a headache and feel stressed and irritated, ask Him to talk to you about why you end up in that place, every Friday evening. Ask about how He would have you conduct your week differently so you can avoid the headache. A good deal of the time, our healing is held up because we don't want to make changes that will benefit us—because our Mind or our Heart want to think or believe something that clearly is not working for our Body's benefit. Breaking that cycle requires that *all* of our board members submit to the leading of the Holy Spirit CEO, and learn to care for the Body the way He intended.

chapter nine

The Holy Spirit and Rightful CEO

"I have spoken these things to you while I remain with you. But the Counselor, the Holy Spirit—the Father will send Him in My name—will teach you all things, and remind you of everything I have told you" (John 14:25-26, HCSB).

Journal Entry, 26th August, 2003: *"...Lord, I can't find You in the crowd. I catch glimpses—I want to see **You**—unobstructed and unhindered...show me where You are. Let the crowd take care of themselves. Let my only concern be You...*

"One of the questions for discussion at group today was, "Have you learned to hear the still quiet voice of the Lord?" I think I was on the path to recognizing Your voice, a long time ago. These days, I think I recognize a whisper, but then I convince myself that it wasn't really You...

*"I've lost You in the crowd, and I desperately, **desperately** want to find You again!"*

Journal Entry, 8th May, 2007: *"...In this picture of my Boardroom, You are sitting in the middle of the board table with Your legs crossed, elbows on Your knees, and chin in Your hands...You're just sitting there like You're waiting for something... What **are** You waiting for?*

"FOR SOMEONE TO ASK FOR HELP."

There is a well-known scripture in Revelation 3:20 that says, *"Listen! I stand at the door and knock. If anyone hears my voice and opens the door, I will come in and have dinner with him, and he with Me"* (HCSB). We often think, and not incorrectly, that this is an invitation from the Lord. There is, however, a two-step process to the verse that we tend to overlook because of its simplicity.

For the Lord to enter in, we must accept His invitation, but that is only half of the answer. We must answer His entreaty with an invitation of our own—"Won't you come in?" Otherwise, all we can expect out of this divine relationship is to conduct the occasional chat with Him as He stands on the front porch.

If we do not invite Him in, He will not come in. The verse does not say, "Behold! I take a running start at your door to knock it down! Better get out of my way!" He doesn't barge His way in nor force or coerce you to do anything. That's the amazing thing about *free will*—we have the choice of whether or not to come to God, listen to Him, and to obey what He says. We also have the choice on whether or not to let Him in.

Love Versus Control

There is a line in the movie Bruce Almighty that captures this concept well. If you know the movie, you will know that Bruce (played to hilarious and irreverent perfection by Jim Carey) thought he could do a better job of being God than what God was doing. So, God (played by Morgan Freeman) magnanimously decides to let Bruce have a go at being God.

There are just two rules that Bruce must uphold; He can't tell anyone he's God, and he's not allowed to mess with free will. Bruce is confident (some might call him cocky) that this God gig will be a piece of cake until he runs into problems with his girlfriend. When she leaves him, believing he is quite messed up (which he was…let's be honest),

Bruce has a conversation with God and asks him, "How do you *make* someone love you without affecting free will?" God's answer, "When you figure that one out, let me know!"

God doesn't want to *make* us love Him. He wants us to love Him *of our own free will*. In order for us to choose to love Him, we first have to choose to give Him an audience, but often we forget to give Him the floor. Learning about our boardroom, all the different members, their God-given roles and unregenerate proclivities only gets us so far. Understanding how our boardroom operates is of no help at all if we don't subsequently learn to submit to the Holy Spirit CEO.

We often get ourselves so tied up and cornered into our own way of thinking that we mistakenly believe that nothing can be done about our circumstances. We forget Philippians 4:13, *"For I can do everything through Christ, who gives me strength"* (NLT). We forget Jesus' own words in Luke 18:27, *"What is impossible for people is possible with God"* (NLT). When we are at the end of ourselves, He is waiting for us to ask for help. He always was waiting; we just have to learn to ask earlier!

Here is the expanded version of the above journal entry, which gives you an idea of how this can happen and how the Holy Spirit CEO can bring us back around to His way of thinking.

Journal Entry, 8th May 2007: S: *"You're sitting in the middle of the boardroom table with Your legs crossed, elbows on Your knees, and Your chin in Your hands. At first, it looked like You were fading in and out of sight—like You were invisible, or holographic or something. Why?"*

"WHO ELSE IS IN YOUR BOARDROOM?"

S: *"Fear…?"*

"DON'T GUESS. TELL ME WHAT YOU SEE."

S: *"Lightening—flashes of light that light up everything and cast it in shadows. I can't clearly see what else…its almost as if each board member is being told what to think and how to behave. Like something is controlling them—a puppet master of some sort. You're just sitting there like You're waiting for something. What are You waiting for?"*

"FOR SOMEONE TO ASK FOR HELP."
S: "But they're all so controlled—how can they?"
"YOU CAN SPEAK."
S: "But I can't make them listen!"
"I'M LISTENING…"
S: "True…so what's going on?"
"EACH BOARD MEMBER IS SEEKING ITS OWN COMFORT."
"THE BODY INDULGES IN CREATURE COMFORTS AND EATS FOR PLEASURE RATHER THAN NUTRITION."
"YOUR MIND SEEKS SOLACE IN FICTION RATHER THAN MY WORD."
"THE CONSCIENCE FEELS BETTER POINTING OUT THE DOWNFALL OF OTHERS RATHER THAN DOING ITS OWN JOB."
"THE WILL WON'T EXERT ITSELF FOR ANYTHING OTHER THAN WHAT THE HEART, MIND, AND BODY PROMISE WILL BE OF PERSONAL BENEFIT."
*"THE HEART—WELL, THE HEART **THINKS** IT'S ON THE RIGHT TRACK BUT IT FAILS TO RECOGNIZE ITS BINDINGS."*
*"YOUR EMOTIONS ARE JUST RESPONDING TO THE SORE SPOTS IN THE HEART, AND YOU KEEP DOING THE ONLY THING YOU BELIEVE YOU **CAN** DO, WHICH IS TO TRY TO GET THROUGH TO EVERYONE ELSE."*
S: "How did we become so dysfunctional?"
"FEAR IS INSIDIOUS. IT SNEAKS UP ON YOU."
S: "Are we tied up because we have given in to fear?"
"PARTLY. YOU'RE ALSO TIED UP BECAUSE YOU ASKED TO BE BOUND."
S: "How did we ask for it?!"
"BY NOT SEEKING ME AND MY PROTECTION FROM FEAR."

At this point, my Heart wants in on the conversation—curiosity gets the better of it, and it jumps in…

H: *"So…we're bound by default? Fear got in because we didn't see it coming, and so we didn't ask You to protect us from it?"*

"YES."

H: *"It doesn't really seem fair…"*

S: *"But—we were told to be on our guard and we weren't. We let it in."*

H: *"Like Adam letting the serpent into the Garden of Eden?"*

S: *"Yeah. We sinned because of what we **didn't** do—we didn't ask for His protection, **and** we've sinned because of what we **did** do—gave into fear and let it take control."*

H: *"So how do we get rid of it?"*

"BY DOING WHAT WASN'T DONE, AND BY UNDOING WHAT WAS DONE. FULL SUBMISSION OF ALL MEMBERS IS REQUIRED BECAUSE ALL ARE BOUND…"

My boardroom became bound by fear essentially because I hadn't been paying attention. I think it is worth stating that, as with any relationship, there are many things that go unsaid in conversations that both parties understand. All those unsaid understandings are hard to communicate in one excerpt. Allow me to try and bring some clarity to the conversation that is happening here.

When the Lord says to me that I am bound because I didn't seek His protection from fear, there is a back story that goes with that comment that my Heart and my Human Spirit immediately recognized and grabbed hold of. The Lord had been speaking to me a lot at that time, about taking refuge in Him, being on guard against anything that would take my attention away from seeking refuge in Him. So, the moment He said, "By not seeking Me and my protection," I knew exactly to what He was referring. I was not being reprimanded for not acting on something of which I was unaware. He was reminding me of something I should have been aware of and pointing out that I let my guard down.

There were many things happening in this season of my life. I had become distracted by a lot of really good things. Ministry, friends, church happenings, small groups, and more ministry were all distracting me. What I failed to realize was that I was choosing what to do, and what not to do, based on fear—fear of what people would or wouldn't say, or fear of what the repercussions would be if I didn't do certain things. I was saying *yes* to a bunch of stuff to which I should have been saying *no*. At the same time I was saying *no* to many things that would have been beneficial to my spiritual growth had I exercised the courage to say *yes*.

How the Board Relates to the CEO

Getting each of the board members to submit to the Holy Spirit CEO was tricky, but not impossible. The more time you spend "paying attention" to your board room, the quicker you will begin discerning which board member has the problem, and getting them to go to the Holy Spirit CEO for a conversation.

As in any corporate setting, the knowledge that a conversation is going to be awkward does not mean that the conversation should not occur. Sometimes we are fully aware that the conversation is going to be difficult. For the times we are not aware of the difficulty, the good news is that we are dealing with a loving and gentle God who will lead us into the truth of what we need to know without pulling the rug out from under us.

The biggest stumbling block I found in this area, initially, was the time it required. There is no five-minute quick fix for a dysfunctional boardroom. Sometimes I became impatient with the process; I often looked for ways to shortcut the pathways that the Lord would lay out for me. Learning to trust Him in His capacity as CEO was exhausting at times, because I would forget from one time to the next, that His way really *did* work better—even if it seemed that it made things worse before they improved!

I became excruciatingly familiar with Proverbs 3:5-6; *"Trust in the Lord with all your Heart, and do not rely on your own understanding; think about Him in all your ways, and He will guide you on the right paths" (HCSB)*. In actuality, it could be said that I fully believed that verse to say something more along the lines of, "Trust in the Lord when it suits you and if it is compatible with your own understanding. In all your ways, acknowledge that He *might* know better than you and direct your own paths…just remember to give Him the credit when it works out!"

My pride and my self-righteousness got (gets) the better of me on many occasions. I had numerous conversations with the Lord about pride—how to recognize it, how to deal with it, how to protect my Heart and Mind from its effects and how to repent of it.

I am reluctant to admit that I have had to revisit *that* lesson many times over. I wish I could tell you that it was a walk in the park. I guess it sort of was—a walk through Central Park, at nighttime with no protection and a huge target on my back to which the enemy could take aim. He rarely missed. Remember in chapter six when we talked about being empowered by the thing to which we surrender? When I surrender to the lies, pride tells me that I'm right, entitled to judge others, above reproach, and unaffected by sin. Those lies empower me to be right, entitled, "holier-than-thou" and blissfully unaware of my own shortcomings. I shudder at the thought that I can be like that, but I am comforted and encouraged by the thought that surrendering to the Holy Spirit CEO can restore to me the humility, compassion, patience, and kindness that better suit a child of God.

The Holy Spirit (CEO) was sent to us to *"lead us into all truth"* (See John 16:13). The Holy Spirit CEO will only tell us what He hears Jesus say: *"All that belongs to the Father is Mine; this is why I said, 'The Spirit will tell you whatever He receives from me.'" (John 16:15, NLT)*. Our heavenly Father is after our Heart. He wants, above all else, a Heart connection and an intimate relationship with us. He will not mess with our free will to get our Heart. He wants to win it, fair and square.

At the end of the movie, Bruce Almighty, Bruce makes his peace with God and reconciles with his girlfriend. He learned the important lesson that *God is not about controlling us.* He is all about loving us—warts and all.

The outcome of my conversation with Him about my boardroom being controlled by fear is still being worked out. I do believe that we can be completely free from fear—perfect love drives out all fear. Fear is insidious. I have learned, with varying degrees of success, to be ever vigilant against that foe.

Engaging the "Difficult" Members

The Human Spirit, being the Personal Assistant to the Holy Spirit, is usually the first to speak up and begin a conversation with the Holy Spirit CEO. That conversation sometimes begins because my Heart is having an issue or asking a question of Him, but not always.

Sometimes, it is as simple as my Human Spirit engaging with the Holy Spirit CEO in conversation—a question like, "What is it You want me to know, today, Lord?" is all I need to get started. Sometimes I will inquire about a picture that He has shown me, or a situation that has bothered me, or a reaction I had in a certain set of circumstances. My Heart will rarely jump right into a conversation with the Holy Spirit CEO because, nine out of ten times, it is hurting; and yes, quite possibly it is sulking over the issue that brought me to Him in the first place. My Human Spirit, working under the direction of the Holy Spirit, labors to allow my Heart to arrive at a place where it feels safe enough and confident enough to converse with the Lord on its own terms.

Because it is my Human Spirit that must persuade my Heart (or any of the other board members) to speak with the Holy Spirit CEO, it is of great importance that I learn to feed and nurture my Human Spirit to keep it healthy and connected to God. Expecting my Human Spirit to perform its job on a diet of popular Christian music and a few hours at church each week doesn't make the grade. As I have already shared, I had to seriously consider how to reinstate the health and well-being, as well as the authority, of my Human Spirit among the board members.

Additionally, finding that my Heart was sometimes so hesitant to talk to Jesus about its concerns (aka "junk") was a shock to me. I thought that my Heart would automatically be drawn to Him, and I was astonished to realize that a big part of the reason why I found it so difficult to pray, much of the time, was that *my Heart wasn't in it*.

Have you ever felt like your prayers were just bouncing off the ceiling? I've been there, more times than I care to admit; but once I learned that it actually didn't take much to get my Heart engaged in the process of prayer, my prayer life got a shot in the arm!

The Heart needs to be heard, but it should not always be obeyed. What does that mean, exactly?

Remember the story about Billy and Johnny in chapter four? Learning to hear from our Heart and to decipher the emotional messages it sends us is very much like dealing with a hurting child. Whether the hurt is physical or emotional, the child wants to feel validated or heard. Agreeing with the child's assessment of the situation is not the goal of the exercise. Carrying out the child's wishes against the perpetrator of the situation is not usually necessary either. Hearing the child's concerns and allowing that child to feel that his or her concerns are important to you is the goal. A child will learn to trust the adult who listens to them and will be happy to follow the direction of that adult; even if the outcome is different from the one the child initially requested.

Our Heart is no different. If our Heart trusts Jesus, it will be happy to take direction from Him. Sometimes, though, our Heart does not trust Him. Here is where our Human Spirit comes into play, as I shared earlier in this chapter.

The outworking of this process took some dedication and perseverance, in the beginning, but the more your Heart works with your

Human Spirit and the Holy Spirit CEO to work through its issues, the quicker the process becomes.

Consequently, many of my early boardroom sessions began with my Human Spirit getting its marching orders from the Lord and then going to my Heart (or any of the other board members) for a conversation.

Do you remember, in the chapter on the Human Spirit, how I wrote about my Heart being bound by self-righteousness, pride, and fear? My Heart told my Human Spirit to, "Tell someone who cares!" so my Human Spirit went straight to the Lord for further instruction. Let's pick up the conversation from the point where the Lord directed my Human Spirit in what to pray for, and how to "fight for my Heart." Before long, my Heart was conversing attentively with the Holy Spirit CEO and could receive the healing and direction that it needed to move forward.

Journal Entry, 7th November, 2008: S: *"So, what do I need to do?"*
"BIND THEM"
S: *"Can't I just cast them out? Get rid of them?"*
"YOU BIND THEM. SHE CASTS THEM OUT."
S: *"Okay then—fear, pride, and self-righteousness, in the Name of Jesus Christ I bind you and command you to let go of my Heart! (Was that okay?)"*
"YES, DEARHEART! NOW CONTINUE…"
H: *"What did you just do?"*
S: *"Only what He told me to do."*
H: *"Which was what?"*
S: *"Bind that which was holding you and release you from it."*
H: *"Wow. Thanks. Did you get rid of them?"*
S: *"No—apparently, you have to do that."*
H: *"Me? Why?"*
S: *"Because He wouldn't let me cast them out. He said you have to… so you can recognize them and deal with them. I think you have to look at them and name them…you know them.*

H: "Yeah. I know them. Fear, pride, and self-righteousness. Why do they keep coming back?"

"BECAUSE YOU ALLOW THEM BACK."

H: "At what point did I do that?"

"YOU LET DOWN YOUR GUARD. THEY CREPT IN, IN DISGUISE."

H: "What were they disguised as this time?"

"CAUTION, RIGHTEOUSNESS, AND SELF-RESPECT."

H: "All quite noble. How do I tell the difference?"

"LET'S START WITH FEAR VERSUS CAUTION—FEAR IS ALL-ENCOMPASSING AND PARALYZING. CAUTION JUST HOLDS YOU BACK LONG ENOUGH TO ASSESS THE DANGER."

H: "Obviously, fear doesn't have to paralyze right from the start or it couldn't disguise itself so well as caution...it still has the ability to help me assess danger, but then it keeps me assessing the danger and won't let me move forward."

"RIGHT. SO, WHY DID IT STAY?"

H: "Because I agreed that there was too much danger to move forward, and I let it convince me that, therefore, I **couldn't** move forward…"

The goal of any boardroom conversation, I have found, is to reconnect my Heart to the Holy Spirit CEO. Sometimes my Heart is bound by the results of its own foolish behavior and decisions—such as the choice to partner with pride, self-righteousness, and fear—as shown in the above exchange.

Sometimes, though, my Heart is at the mercy of one of the other board members. Perhaps it might be the Emotions, or the Conscience, or even the Mind that seeks to control the Heart. In those instances, finding the underlying cause of what is going on requires a focused conversation and a good portion of patience!

Last Words

In the opening chapter, I laid out a description of the dysfunctional boardroom. Let's now look at the well-run, highly functional boardroom. The same characters are there, but with very different roles, and with a very different awareness of who is in charge.

The Holy Spirit CEO is present and is very much respected, having been given the authority by everyone in attendance to have the final word.

To the left of the Holy Spirit CEO is the Mind—or the Systems Analyst. Our Mind is a gift of great consequence. Our Mind is designed to think, to analyze all the information we receive, and to interpret it accordingly. Rather than controlling everything, it is meant to measure everything against what the Holy Spirit CEO has sanctioned and present its findings to the other members so that the information can be shared and understood.

Next to the Mind is the Heart—the Record Keeper. Everything that happens, good, bad, or indifferent, is kept, recorded, and filed away by the Heart. This is an important job. Some of what is recorded gets filed in our conscious memory and is easily accessible to all the board members, while some get filed in our subconscious memory and can only be accessed by the Heart and the Holy Spirit CEO.

In the next chair around the table, sit the Emotions. The Emotions are messengers from the Heart. Their role is to bring the message that the Heart sends—anger, sadness, fear, excitement, or whatever it may be—and present that message to the board.

Rather than dominating the boardroom with messages that threaten to overwhelm the meeting, the Emotions are simply there to let the rest of the board know that "a button has been pressed". More accurately, it lets the rest of the board members know that there is something filed in the subconscious memory that relates to this situation. That information may be important to the circumstances at hand or just important to the Heart. Either way, the message is relayed by the Emotions for the immediate *or* future consideration of the board. Often, once the message has been appropriately received, the Emotions settle down and business can resume.

Next, we have the Conscience, whose role is to build character. You could consider the submitted Conscience to be a trusted mentor who can readily spot the conviction of the Holy Spirit CEO. As I shared previously, the Conscience, if ignored, can be a bully but it is extremely valuable as a teacher of character. Once it learns to work with the conviction of the Holy Spirit CEO, it is wise to listen to what the Conscience has to say.

The Will is next at the table and is no longer a floating voter but is the approved Executive Secretary to the Holy Spirit CEO. When the Will is submitted to the Holy Spirit, even if the other board members lapse into dysfunctional behavior, the Will remains strong in its desire and mandate to carry out the will of the Holy Spirit CEO, and eventually the others on the team will learn to respect that determination.

The Body can now assume its rightful position as the Temple of the Holy Spirit, and is respected and cared for, accordingly.

Last, but not least, our Human Spirit steps into the role of Personal Assistant to the Holy Spirit. *"God is Spirit, and those who worship Him must worship Him in **spirit** and in truth…"(John 4:24, HCSB).* *"The Spirit Himself testifies **together with our spirit** that we are God's children…" (Romans 8:16, HCSB).*

Our Human Spirit, working together with God's Holy Spirit, allows Him to lead us into all truth. Our Human Spirit is the connection point between God and us, and it has full authority in the boardroom to call the other members to attention when it is needed.

In this boardroom scenario, intimacy springs up where before there was none. Prayer becomes ingrained into our lifestyle as we learn to converse with God at any time about anything. Almost in spite of ourselves, we find that transformation into His image is taking place with no effort from us to make it so, but by the Power of the Holy Spirit working within us.

My life, and my spiritual life, have changed radically since that journal entry in Easter of 2003. I think it is fortunate that we don't always know exactly what we are asking when we pray the scary prayers. God, in His graciousness, shields us from so much of what we don't know. He leads us gently through the lessons that we must learn along the way. His mercies really are new every morning, and His faithfulness to always lead us into truth is never ceasing.

What I have learned over the years is that there is no limit to His Love. When I began this journey, I was in a place of uncertainty. I was uncertain of who I was because I was uncertain of who God was. I couldn't trust Him, even when I wanted to because I didn't know Him. I didn't even trust myself to try and get to know Him. There were too many conflicting ideas and beliefs fighting for dominance in my boardroom, and I hadn't the first clue as to how to address any of it.

Once I began to identify the members of my boardroom, I found I could more clearly identify the voice of the Holy Spirit. The more I practiced; the easier it got to hear Him above the noise of the outside world and the inner clatter of my own thoughts.

I am still human—I am still visited by condemnation on many occasions, but I do not *wrestle* or *struggle* with it anymore. I have the tools, the knowledge, and the skills to pinpoint it and overcome it because He who is in me (my Holy Spirit CEO) is greater than condemnation, or anything else that the world wants to throw at me. I am confident in who God is, and because of that, I am certain of who I am in Him.

Every day is an adventure waiting to be had with Him! There is always a current testimony, a fresh revelation, a *now* story of what God is doing in my life, and it's exciting, inspiring, encouraging and comforting to know that He really is always *there*.

This loving, gentle, gracious, merciful, and majestic God that we serve just wants our *all*—our intimacy and affection and obedience and devotion. He won't force us to give it. He pursues us relentlessly, never gives up, and is always patiently waiting for us to come to Him to ask for help. Now you are better prepared to go about doing that…

Your CEO has called a meeting; the agenda is clear—it is an agenda of love. Will you attend?

acknowledgements

A book is not written by just one person. The author gets to put their name on the cover and receives all the accolades when the book is complete, but any author worth their salt knows that they are just a small (albeit important) cog in the machine. With that in mind, it is appropriate that I mention some of the people who have given their time, their wisdom, their patience, and their insight over many years. These are the people I have conversed with, wrestled with, lived with, loved, and worked with over the years; they have encouraged me, corrected me, nurtured me, and shaped me; and through the love and commitment they have shown, I have learned much.

So, to the following people, I say "Thank you.":

Susanne and Daniel Fengler—thank you for your obedience and your openness; firstly, in receiving from the Lord this concept of the Boardroom, and secondly, in being so very generous and encouraging in giving it away. You have taught me the valuable truth that when the Holy Spirit teaches me something, it will take root and grow if I give it away. I well remember asking Susanne to come and teach this material to a group of my friends in a neighboring suburb—she graciously declined by looking me in the eye and stating firmly, but with so much love, "*You* teach them!" So, I did.

Fiona, Nic, Libby, Sarah, and Miriam—thank you for having more faith in me than I did myself, and for allowing me to teach you the things the Lord was revealing to me as we worked through the Boardroom material together. This was where it all started. You were the first to tell me I should write a book, and we still hold the record for the longest (continuously) running Boardroom group ever!

Amie—thank you, thank you, thank you for recognizing my hunger and inviting me along to Thursday Group. Your continued investment into me from that time to this has had an impact around the world. You are a world-changer, and I am blessed to call you friend!

To all the ladies at Crossway Baptist Church Thursday Group, 2003—2007: There are too many of you to name, but if you were there, you know who you are. You were a safe place to practice all that we learned together. Thank you for the many birthday blessings, words of encouragement, and prophetic words that were spoken in timid but determined obedience to the promptings of the Holy Spirit. I treasure every word that was given and everyone of you!

To Robin, Lisa, Brenda, and Katrina who encouraged me to share the Boardroom for the first time in the USA…you had faith in this Aussie girl to teach you, and I am humbled by that faith, and excited by the growth you displayed as you learned to trust the Lord in new ways.

To our leadership team, and our dear family at Crossroads Church, Waxhaw, NC. You are truly an amazing and Godly group of believers who daily inspire me to worship harder, pray with more confidence, love unconditionally, and pursue my relationship with our heavenly Father with more fervor. I love living this life with all of you!

To every person that ever conversed with me over a cup of tea, coffee, or hot chocolate, challenging me to dig deeper, press in closer, explore in more detail, or see from a different perspective, and who allowed me to do the same in return—thank you. There are too many of you to name, but you know who you are, and I would not be who I am today without your input and insight.

Jason, Jan, and Jerri—for all your editing and suggestions and encouragement to make this book the best it could be, thank you! Your time, your shared knowledge, and your attention to the details I overlooked have been invaluable, and I am grateful beyond measure.

To my husband Mark, whose vision, drive, endless enthusiasm, and determination has put wings on many of my dreams and aspirations over the years. This book would not be in existence without you; I would not be who I am today without you!

By no means is it redundant or cliché to thank my Lord and Savior. You have been an ever-present friend and confidant. My journey would have been very different without Your constant Presence and Wisdom. Your patience and gentleness with my faltering progress along the way has been a blessing and my continuing joy. There is no One like You, Lord! I am thankful forever that You have made this adventure safe and rewarding and accessible, and I thank You for allowing me the privilege of sharing it with others as I go.

All of these, and many more, have had a hand in the production of this work. They are all a part of this story and have left a lasting impression on my heart. I wrote down all of the words; each of these has had a hand in shaping the message contained in the pages. My heartfelt thanks and gratitude to you all!

OTHER RESOURCES AVAILABLE

Thank you for purchasing Boardroom of the Inner Man!
As part of our commitment to you, we invite you to
take advantage **TODAY** of our
FREE introductory offer:
a one-hour call with Julie.

Our desire is to help you become one of the most influential spiritual leaders in the world.

To learn more about Julie and Mark Appleyard's work with Anothen,
and to access their other resources
or consultancy services:

Visit www.anothen.co

or simply scan the QR Code to get your FREE Introductory call!

www.anothen.co/get-started